Taligent's Guide to Designing Programs

Well-mannered object-oriented design in C++

TALIGENT
PRESS

Addison-Wesley Publishing Company

Reading, Massachusetts   Menlo Park, California   New York
Don Mills, Ontario   Wokingham, England   Amsterdam   Bonn   Sydney
Singapore   Tokyo   Madrid   San Juan   Paris   Seoul   Milan   Mexico City   Taipei

Library of Congress Cataloging-in-Publication Data

Taligent's guide to designing programs : well-mannered object-oriented
   design in C++.
                  p.   cm.
      "Taligent Press."
      Includes index.
      ISBN   0-201-40888-0
      1. Object-oriented programming (Computer science)   2. C++
      (Computer program language)   I. Taligent, Inc.
      QA76.64.T34   1994
      005.2--dc20   94-1186
                                                       CIP

Sponsoring Editor: Martha Steffen
Cover and text design: Taligent Technical Communications Group, Gary Ashcavai
Set in 10 point New Baskerville

2 3 4 5 6 7-CRS-97969594
Second printing, August 1994

Addison-Wesley books are available for bulk purchases by corporations, institutions, and other
organizations. For more information please contact the Corporate, Government and Special Sales
Department at (800) 238-9682.

Taligent's Guide to Designing Programs is a collection of guidelines and conventions that Taligent® engineers follow as they design and build the Taligent Application Environment.

This book is not meant to be read from cover to cover; instead, pick a topic of interest and become familiar with it.

To find an interesting topic, open this book to any chapter, read the annotated Contents, look at only the code samples, or scan the Index.

What's important is to become familiar with the topics so that when you have design questions, you'll know where to look.

BRIEF CONTENTS

CONTENTS

*Taligent architectural goals and the principles that help you design software
more effectively.*

Follow these guidelines as you design individual classes.

*The client interface reflects precisely the information relevant to the client's
problem domain, and no more. Doing this well is key to object-oriented
design.*

*Resources register themselves with services; services should not look for
resources. If you need to use another object, let the client give it to you: don't
find it yourself.*

*All interfaces in the Taligent Application Environment are expressed in
terms of objects, specifically, classes corresponding to the abstractions that a
developer must deal with.*

*An invariant is an assertion about an object's internal state that is helpful
in making sure that the object transitions from one valid state to another,
and meets the behavioral promises in its interface.*

*The C++ typing features are a great help in defining the interface to a class,
but the entire definition of a class can't be expressed in the C++ definition.
For a class definition to be complete, you must define its constructors and
destructor, copy constructor, and assignment operators.*

4 Taligent environment programming conventions

5   Taligent environment programming tips and techniques 91

A

Class templates 115

Template implementations are hard to maintain because they get compiled into your client's code. Templates also, by their very nature, tend to bloat the resulting object code. This guide provides design standards and conventions to increase code maintainability, and to reduce the memory footprint.

Definitions and conventions 115

A class template is the definition of the template for the class; a specialized class is a class produced by invoking the template. By convention, end class-template names with prepositions. Also, place the noninline class-template method implementations in a separate include file.

Sharing class template implementations 117

To be reusable, the implementation class deals with objects at the level common to all types that your template can be instantiated with. Any implementation-hiding class template design depends upon the specifics of your code.

Sharing the implementation through private inheritance 123

This technique uses private inheritance to share the implementation class between multiple specializations of the template.

Sharing the implementation by delegating to a member 130

An alterative to private inheritance is to delegate the implementation to a member. This technique usually leads to cleaner code than achieved by using private inheritance.

Bibliography 137

In addition to listing the documents cited in this book, here are other books you can read for further study.

Index 141

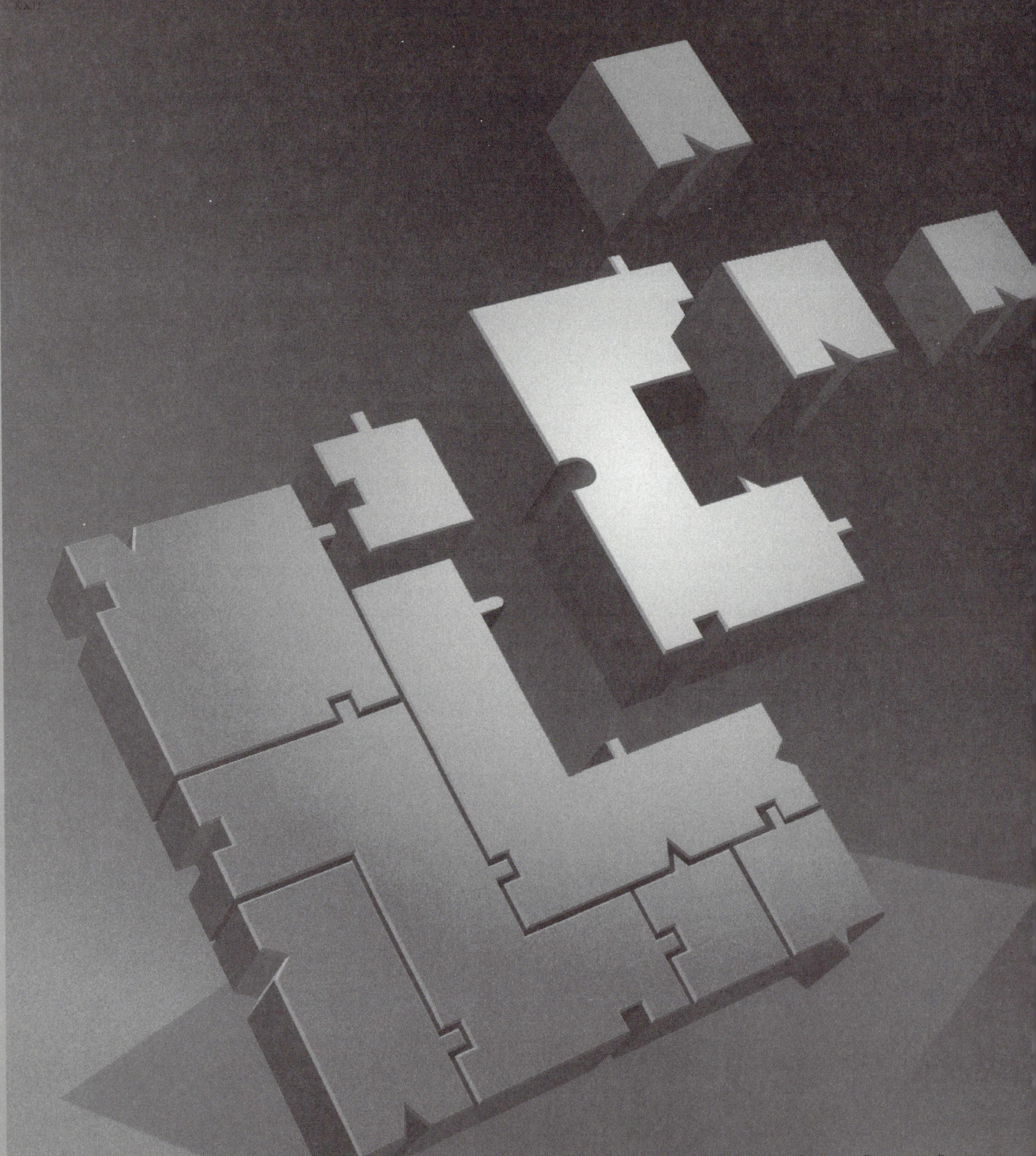

PREFACE

If you browse the computer section of any technical bookstore, you'll find many good books offering advice on how to do object-oriented design—books dealing both with general design principles and with design principles specific to C++. Why then does the industry need another book, one targeted not only to a specific language (C++), but to a specific system?

My experience has been that object-oriented design is best learned from using it to actually build systems. The style guidelines and design rules in *Taligent's Guide to Designing Programs* come from years of that kind of experience, building large object-oriented C++ systems in the Taligent® environment. If you plan to develop for Taligent environments, this book will provide you with an understanding of the philosophy underlying Taligent's designs, and the way in which to fit your own work into Taligent's environments. If your interest is simply in object-oriented design and C++, then my hope is that this book will benefit you by showing the experiences of one company.

This book grew from an internal style guide I wrote, which Taligent uses to develop its products, to train engineers, and to orient Taligent early developers to the Taligent system. These guidelines, like most, are based partly on empirical heuristics, and partly on principles. Although the focus has always been specifically on the writing of Taligent software, much of what we have learned is applicable not only to Taligent, but to any C++ system.

It is important for Taligent to have a consistent style of design across the many components that make up our systems, but you may find a different style that works well for you. We are interested in hearing about your experiences—if you have comments, please send them to Internet: Taligent_DTS@Taligent.com or CompuServe: 766711,1260.

This book assumes that you have a working knowledge of C++ and of object-oriented design. If you are just starting out on either, you will find several useful introductory books listed in the Bibliography.

Acknowledgments

Although the list is too lengthy to present here, I would like to thank those individuals, both at Taligent and other companies, whose contributions and reviews helped make this book possible. I'd also like to thank Taligent's Technical Communications department for taking my internal style guide and transforming it, over several editions, into something more suitable for publication.

Cupertino, California   David Goldsmith

David Goldsmith is a Senior Scientist at Taligent, Inc., where he has contributed to the architecture, design, and consistency of the Taligent Application Environment. Previously, he led work on early versions of the MacApp® application framework at Apple Computer.

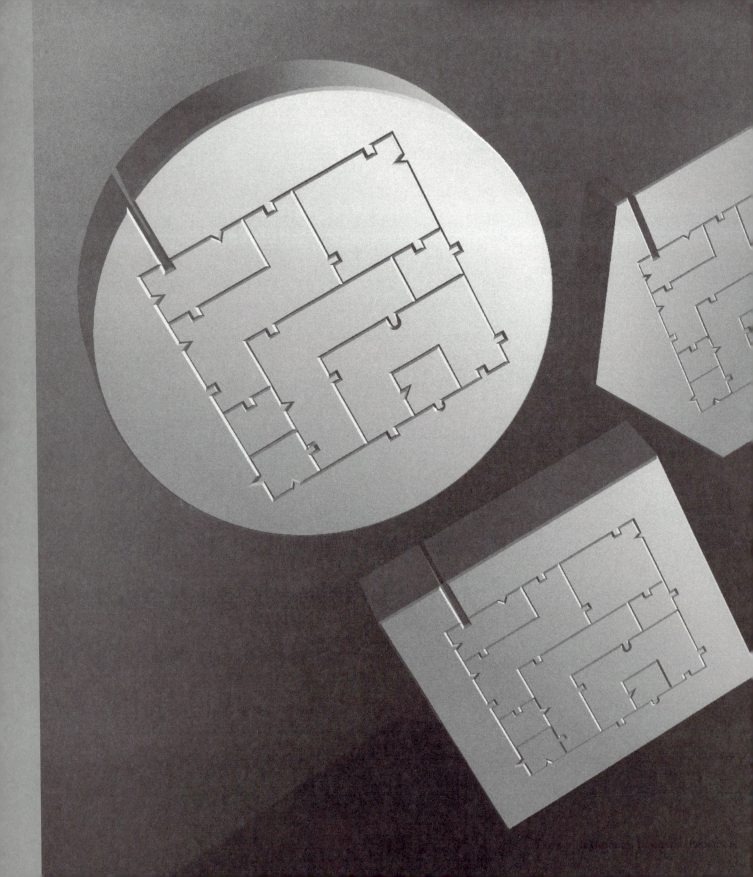

CHAPTER 1

INTRODUCTION

The Taligent Application Environment system software platform introduces a powerful new programming model and architecture that enables developers to build exciting applications for a variety of platforms.

ARCHITECTURAL GOALS

To achieve its overall design goals, Taligent established several fundamental architectural principles for the Taligent Application Environment:

- Ensure that the Taligent Application Environment is highly portable to new architectures, that it is fully international, and that it encapsulate environmental assumptions—enabling software developers to be flexible in reacting to changes in customer requirements, market conditions, and new technology.
- Ensure that the environment and APIs are consistent, coherent, and clear.
- Encourage system encapsulation through all service layers to minimize risk and to allow for parallel development and extension.
- Promote robustness by designing quality into the behavior of the environment, simplifying the coding effort required of developers.

The guidelines in this book helped Taligent meet its architectural goals for the Taligent Application Environment. Becoming familiar with them will provide you with a better understanding of the design and coding choices made for the Taligent Application Environment, enabling you to more effectively design software for it or other object-oriented systems.

OBJECT-ORIENTED ARCHITECTURE

The object-oriented design of the Taligent Application Environment supports its architectural goals. Some of the key features of this design are explored here.

All interfaces are expressed through objects

To provide the most flexibility, the client interface to services should be through classes and the objects of those classes. Achieving this flexibility means that, among other things, messages, file formats, and data formats should never be defined as attributes of the interface. Although all these services can be used in the implementation of other services, they should never form part of another service's interface.

But simply using objects is not enough: to perform well, objects must be correctly defined. In the Taligent Application Environment objects are defined in terms not of the implementation, but of the abstraction presented to the client. It is tempting to pile everything into the class interface, but resist this urge. The key is to design the class from the client's point of view, by asking these important object-oriented design questions:

- What are the entities involved?
- What do I need to know about them?
- What operations can I perform on them?

For more information, see "Reflect the client's view" on page 7 and "Express all interfaces through objects" on page 9.

Commonality is managed through inheritance

Commonality in software systems has traditionally been managed through the commonality of implementation. For example, UNIX® systems manage devices by making everything look like a block device or a character device. Device-specific features are provided through extensions.

A better method is provided by type inheritance. A base class defines an abstraction, and thus an interface, common to many objects. Specific objects then derive from that base class, declaring themselves to be subtypes. These objects implement those features unique to themselves, as well as those of the common protocol. Several levels of abstract base classes thus yield successively more refined points of commonality. Additionally, to support more than one shared protocol, objects can inherit from multiple base classes. (See "Use type inheritance to share protocol" on page 13.)

The benefit to clients is that they need only deal with the level of detail required by talking to the abstract base class and by making themselves independent of the details of the subclasses—allowing the details of the abstract base class to change, or for new subclasses to be added, without breaking existing software.

Note that inheritance of code has nothing to do with type relationships, and should be dealt with by has-a relationships (member objects), private base classes (a special kind of has-a relationship), or protected interfaces. However, it's acceptable and common to inherit both code and type from the same base class.

Objects are leveraged wherever possible

Using an existing object is better than inventing or reinventing a new one. Less code means a smaller memory footprint, yielding better performance; fewer classes means less for the developer to learn; and less to implement means fewer bugs, leading to a more reliable, more robust system. In the Taligent Application Environment, for example, the Collection classes provide a set of tested and debugged data structures that you don't have to write and debug yourself.

Naturally, leveragability does not mean one size always fits all. In another context, speed or space performance might demand use of a custom data structure. That's OK. As Einstein said, "Everything should be made as simple as possible, but not simpler."

Frameworks provide the foundation

Objects and inheritance help insulate clients from assumptions and unnecessary details. But for a developer implementing a derived class, the interface encapsulates assumptions about the object, but not assumptions about the interactions between objects. This problem can be solved by frameworks—sets of object-oriented classes that are designed to work together.

Taligent believes that frameworks provide the foundation for exploiting object-oriented technology. Frameworks provide an infrastructure that decreases the amount of code that a programmer must develop, test, and debug. Developers write only the code necessary to extend or control the framework's behavior to suit the requirements of a specific application.

Frameworks also allow two subsystems to interact while protecting them from knowledge of each other (they need know only about the framework); whereas a class interface only protects the client from the implementation of the provider. So frameworks not only provide predesigned sets of classes, but also encapsulate details in a way that lets multiple system components be connected together, a feature which individual classes cannot manage.

The Taligent Application Environment uses frameworks extensively, providing application-level frameworks for text and graphics editing, as well as underlying support frameworks for networking, device drivers, file system support, and I/O.

Let resources find you

Traditionally, programs have the names of resources or collections of resources built into them; when executed, they then search for these names, whether they will need them or not. A key design principle in the Taligent Application Environment is to "let resources find you." That is, assumptions about where resources come from aren't built into objects that don't need to know. Instead, resources are described as objects, enabling the substitution of equivalent resource objects later on.

Suppose, for example, an object represents a SCSI device. How should that object deal with the SCSI interface? Should it call a function of some SCSI manager? In a system with more than one SCSI bus, such as a personal computer with optional SCSI cards, this represents a problem because the traditional approach assumes only one SCSI manager. The driver that *knows* where to find the SCSI interface can't deal with this situation. The traditional approach forces a complicated fix that makes multiple buses look like one bus.

If the SCSI bus is an object, however, that gets passed to the SCSI device object when it is created, the SCSI device doesn't need knowledge of how to find the resource (the SCSI bus)—it lets the resource find it.

For more information about working with resources, see "Let resources find you" on page 8.

PUTTING IT ALL TOGETHER

Taligent's Guide to Designing Programs is the rule book that Taligent engineers follow as they develop the Taligent Application Environment. Occasionally you will see directions for engineers to consult their architect. In these situations, if you don't have an architect, or if you are the architect, use your best judgement.

As you develop and design your applications, consider these rules for Taligent engineers to be guidelines for you. However, if you are building a program for the Taligent Application Environment, pay close attention to these conventions to better understand the reason behind the implementation, and to help ensure that your application will be compliant with the Taligent environment.

Chapter 2

Object-oriented design guidelines

Object-oriented design requires that you identify the objects in your system, and then design classes to represent them. As a class designer, you have to know the specifics of the class you are designing and be aware of how that class interacts with other classes. The art of good class design comes from experience: this chapter is a collection of the results of many such experiences.

✅ NOTE   Before you begin designing classes, you should have a solid understanding of what classes are and why they are important. If you are new to object-oriented programming, see the Bibliography for introductory books on this subject.

Classes

Underlying the functionality of any application is the quality of its design. When designing an individual class, follow the guidelines outlined in this section.

Reflect the client's view

The *client* is the calling code that uses the services of a class: it calls the public interface. The benefits of object-oriented design come from making an interface reflect the client's view of a class rather than the implementer's view, and from introducing abstractions that simplify the client's work. The client interface should reflect precisely the information relevant to the client's problem domain, and no more. The easiest way to do this is to design classes that correspond to the natural abstractions of a domain. Learning to do this well is key to learning object-oriented design.

Remember that developers of derived classes are also clients, and you should design the interface to simplify their work. Martin Carroll expressed this principle in "Design of the USL Standard Components," *C++ Report,* June 1993: "Contrary to popular belief, it is rarely possible to take an arbitrary class and derive a new, useful, and correct subtype from it unless that subtype is of a specific kind anticipated by the designer of the base class. A given class can be made extensible only in certain directions."

Developers of derived classes are clients too.

Let resources find you

Resources should register themselves with services; services should not go out looking for resources. This approach is bottom-up rather than top-down. At Taligent, the idea of letting resources find you is a fundamental architectural principle.

Whenever possible, resources should register themselves in the Workspace and services should be told what resources to use via choices from the Workspace, so that users need remember only one way to *choose* things. For example, SCSI software would enumerate the devices attached to a SCSI bus and create device drivers for each device. This would happen once at boot time. From then on, the driver, not the SCSI software, provides access to the resources it represents. A SCSI disk, for instance, registers itself as a raw device to allow users to select it for formatting or partitioning.

If the SCSI disk contains volumes, it also registers itself with the File System to allow the volumes to be mounted. The File System in turn registers the new volumes on the desktop to allow users to select or open them. Note that in each case, the services only need to know the minimum information. That is, the File System only needs to know that something is a storage device, not whether it is a disk, tape, SCSI, or whatever. And the Workspace only needs to know that something is a resource. In the same way, when that resource is selected, the application only needs to know it is a storage device.

A similar example is a SCSI scanner application that looks on the SCSI bus and uses the first scanner it finds. If you have two scanners with different capabilities that you want to use alternately, you're out of luck, because the assumption built into the application is that there is only one scanner.

In the Taligent Application Environment, the scanner application waits for the user to tell it which scanner to use; the scanner might not even be on a SCSI bus. You don't have to rewrite the application to support a scanner that uses some other connection technique: knowledge of how to talk to the scanner is built into the scanner object that is handed to the application.

If you need to use another object, let the client give it to you—don't find it yourself.

Express all interfaces through objects

Almost all interfaces in the Taligent Application Environment are expressed as objects, specifically classes, which correspond to the abstractions that a developer must deal with. Interfaces should not be expressed by struct's, dictionaries, arrays, or any other kind of data structure. You can use these data structures in the interface (as function arguments, for example), but they can't *embody* the interface. Parameter blocks in the Macintosh® operating system are an example of a data structure that embodies the interface.

Avoid using global variables or functions in an interface. Global variables that are really constants are exceptions, as are overloaded operators; for symmetry, the latter must sometimes be global friend functions rather than member functions.

Functions should be members of some class: either regular members, if they can be characterized as an operation on some object, or static members, if they don't apply to one object in particular.

Avoid objects or classes that *do not* correspond to concepts the developer must deal with. A common example is classes whose name contains "Manager" and of which there is only one in a given application or task. These are really modules that have been turned into classes (see "Modulitis" on page 23); they do not make good objects. Usually, their member functions should be dispersed among other classes, either as regular members or as static members. If you have an object that communicates with a server, the object should not be visible in your interface: the existence of servers should *never* be visible in class interfaces (except for those used to implement servers).

Avoid using types that are not objects to represent abstractions that should be objects. One good example of this is ID types; other examples from the Macintosh OS include refNums and resource IDs. The problem with these ID types is that they represent an abstraction, but there is no object.

In the Taligent Application Environment kernel interface, task IDs are replaced by task handle objects. It's still possible to get the task ID for informational purposes, but it has been supplanted by the object as the primary identifier. Similarly, the Window Server uses unique IDs to identify system windows internally, but these IDs aren't visible in the client interface to the Window Server: instead, the client creates system window objects.

Preserve class invariants

An *invariant* is an assertion about an object's internal state. Such assertions are helpful in making sure that the object transitions from one valid state to another and that it meets the behavioral promises of its interface.

To preserve class invariants:

- Know the invariants in a class you design.
- Only allow an invariant to be invalid internally as long as it does not become visible outside the implementation of the class.
- Do not leave invariants invalid for too long.

A good Taligent illustration of all three points is TStream, which encapsulates a concept of a logical end of stream. The invariant is simply that the class represents the correct logical end of stream.

The inline write functions of TStream modify the current position in the stream without checking the logical end. Thus, the class must *catch up* whenever it next gets a chance (that is, when a virtual function gets called). TStream must then infer the new logical end from the new stream position and other data members. If the computation is not performed immediately, that information can change again, and the new logical end will not be correctly computed.

In summary, learn what your invariants are and strive to keep them correct. The Assert function from the Test framework is very helpful. It allows you to test invariants when testing is turned on, but skips the check otherwise. If even that is too expensive, you can conditionally compile your assertions for debugging.

Object-oriented design with C++

In addition to general object-oriented principles, the Taligent Application Environment implements several design principles specific to C++.

C++ doesn't express full object interface

Although the strong typing features of C++ are a great help in defining the interface to a class, the entire definition of a class can't be expressed in the C++ class definition. The following important aspects (among others) of a class interface can't be adequately expressed in C++:

Class semantics—Not all of the semantic constraints on an object can be expressed through the C++ type system.

Concurrency—The behavior of an object in the presence of multiple threads of execution can't be expressed in C++.

Storage management—If an object has specific storage management semantics, they can't be expressed through the class definition.

Special conventions can help to document all these facets of a class in the class definition, but the compiler certainly can't use that information to check your code. Many semantic constraints can only be expressed in human language.

C++ requires definition of special member functions

For a class definition to be complete, you must define its constructor(s) and destructor, copy constructor, and assignment operators. If you don't define these special members, the compiler will, and it can generate them as inlines (which you want to avoid) or make incorrect assumptions about your class structure. If you don't want to allow clients to assign your class or return it from functions, make the copy constructor and assignment operators `private` with no implementation; this keeps the compiler from generating them for you.

Constructors and destructor—Every class should have a destructor and at least one constructor, even if they do nothing or are defined to do nothing. Be explicit; do not leave this up to the compiler.

Copy constructor—The copy constructor for TFoo is of the form `TFoo(const TFoo&)` or `TFoo(TFoo&)`. This constructor defines the behavior of your class when it is passed by value as an argument, returned by value from a function, or used to initialize one instance with the value of another. You must define this constructor so that your objects are copied properly; otherwise, the compiler generates a default inline version for you.

Assignment operator—The assignment operator (`operator=`) is called when one instance of your class is assigned to another; if you don't define it, the compiler generates a default inline version for you. If you allocate subsidiary data structures on the heap or consume any other kind of shared resource, you need to define an assignment operator and a copy constructor. The compiler doesn't define assignment operators if you declare an assignment operator with argument type of `TFoo`, `TFoo&`, or `const TFoo&`.

If you let the compiler generate your copy constructor or assignment operator, at least insert a commented declaration:

Include to show that you didn't forget it

```
// TFoo& operator=(const TFoo&);        // Use default version.
```

Also remember that this constitutes an inline declaration; therefore, if you ever want to allow for a nondefault implementation, you must define these special members explicitly. See "Inline functions" on page 62.

Streaming operators—Although streaming operators (`operator<<=` and `operator>>=`) are not special members in the C++ sense, many of the same considerations apply. The compiler does not generate them for you, but the base class' operators will be inherited (if your base class has them) and might not do the right thing.

ABSTRACT BASE CLASSES

Classes that act as base classes and not meant to be instantiated are called *abstract base classes*. Many classes in the Taligent Application Environment, such as TStream, fall into this category. If you have an abstract base class, use two techniques to make that clear:

Make abstract base class constructors protected to ensure that only a derived class can call the constructor, and so that clients can't try to create an object of that class.

✅ NOTE   Although you can make destructors private or protected to prevent stack allocation, do not make abstract base class destructors private or protected unless you don't want clients to delete an object given a pointer to a base class. This isn't usually the case. See "Control class access" on page 107 for more information.

Use pure virtual functions in your abstract class for those functions that must be overridden by derived classes. For example, before you can create a concrete class (one that can be instantiated), you must override this pure virtual function:

```
class TAbstract {
public:
    virtual void MustOverride() = 0;
};
```

For more information about virtual functions, see "Virtual functions" on page 66.

✅ NOTE   An abstract base class can itself be derived from another class, which might or might not be abstract itself.

INHERITANCE

There are two forms of inheritance in C++: *type inheritance* and *implementation inheritance*. In both forms of inheritance, a derived class can share or override behavior inherited from a base class. However, use type inheritance only when it is necessary for a derived class to inherit type information as well. The primary reason to inherit type information is to allow for polymorphism.

Express type inheritance by deriving a class from a public base class; express implementation inheritance by deriving a class from a private or protected base class. Strict guidelines for choosing the correct form of inheritance are described in this section.

Use type inheritance to share protocol

Use public base classes or public derivation whenever a collection of classes shares protocol in common. The only reason for a base class to be public is so that a pointer or reference to the derived class can be converted into a pointer or reference to the base class. The most important reason to perform these conversions is to allow for *polymorphism* (for example, a function that expects a `Base&` is handed a `Derived&` instead). Polymorphism occurs when a collection of related classes can be used via the protocol they all have in common. This allows one component of a system to deal with other components at the highest level of abstraction possible (the base class) and ignore any irrelevant details (of the derived class).

Type inheritance is also known as *subtyping*; deriving a class from a public base class states that the new class is a subtype. This statement places important constraints on the base class and the derived class. If these constraints are not met, serious errors can occur later. Compilers can't catch many of these errors.

If you want to share only portions of a base class' protocol, make the class private and reexport the members you want to make public (or factor that partial protocol out into a separate base). Use public base classes only when you need polymorphism.

Use implementation inheritance to override behavior

Use private and protected base classes or private and protected derivation to inherit behavior or override it when you don't need to inherit public protocol. Implementation inheritance is often appropriate for inheriting from a framework to override behavior. For example, MRemoteCaller and MRemoteDispatcher in the Taligent Client/Server framework are usually inherited as protected base classes.

When a derived class inherits from a private or protected base class, the derived class has access to all the members of the base, but they are not publicly exported as members of the derived class. For clients, it also means that the derived class is not treated as a subtype of the base class, and no automatic conversions are performed for function arguments or assignments. However, this is only true outside the derived class; within the derived class, the behavior is exactly as if the base class had been declared public.

✅ NOTE   C++ lets you reexport public members of private or protected bases via access control declarations.

As with type inheritance, if you want to share only portions of a base class' protocol, make the class private and reexport the members you want to make public. If a class is used by another class purely in a client relationship, that class should be a member rather than a private or protected base class. Use private or protected base classes only when behavior is inherited or overridden, as in a framework.

Use public base classes only when you need polymorphism.

Design the interfaces between the base and derived classes

Design the interface between a base class and its derived classes just as carefully as the class' interface to clients; it's the contract between the base and derived classes. If this interface is not designed properly, it can lead to violating the type-subtype relationship, which can cause very obscure problems. It can also violate encapsulation of the base class.

The protected portion of the class interface can only be accessed by derived classes. This feature is helpful but can't express the totality of the relationship between a class and its derived classes. Other important factors include *which* functions might and might not be overridden, and *how* they must behave. It is also crucial to consider the relationship between member functions; some of them might need to be overridden in groups to preserve the class' semantics.

The bottom line is this: design your interface to derived classes so that a derived class that uses every supported aspect of that interface (including overriding virtual functions) doesn't compromise the integrity of your public interface. Because C++ can't express the complete interface to derived classes, it is quite easy for a developer who derives a class from yours to violate your class invariants no matter what you do. Make it clear through your interface and documentation how to make a derived class that preserves those invariants.

Expected calls

A simple example of not preserving the base class invariants is when a derived class overrides a function that the base class is counting on the derived class calling. If the derived class doesn't call the base class function, or calls it incorrectly, the base class' invariants are violated and unpredictable results can occur.

You can avoid this problem by making the function in question a *hook* for derived classes to override, and moving the *inherited* version into the code that calls the hook. This only works for one level of derivation; overriding the same function at multiple levels is error prone. Hook functions are the cleanest way to interact with derived classes. For more information, see "Virtual functions" on page 66.

Group override

Sometimes a base class requires that you override virtual functions in groups; correct interaction between the base and its derived classes requires that you override all of the functions in a group together.

This is why a base class designer must make it very clear *how* its virtual functions can be overridden, not just *whether* they can be. Keep in mind that just because a function is virtual does not mean you can override it (see "Virtual functions" on page 66).

Getters and setters

Get and set functions should not be virtual unless they are used by the class that defines them. If the base class does direct field access, you usually can't override the get and set functions correctly. Suppose a derived class overrides a set function so that it can update its own information whenever the base class information is updated. But, if the base class changes the corresponding field directly, a derived class never gets notified and its information becomes stale.

A common practice is to make get functions nonvirtual and set functions virtual. This makes internal access fast, but gives subclasses a chance to react to changes.

✅ NOTE   An example of where this rule of thumb is intentionally violated is a class with a write-only attribute. If the data member being changed can't be read through the class interface (for example, a cache), it is acceptable for the class to set it directly even if there is a virtual interface function that also sets it. However, this is rather unusual; in most cases, if you do not use your own virtual get and set functions you're making a mistake.

What this amounts to is, don't assume that putting `virtual` or `protected` in front of your member functions defines the interface to derived classes. That interface must be as carefully designed and documented as the client interface.

Guarantee use of derived classes as arguments

Any function that accepts a reference or pointer to an object of a given class must be prepared to receive a derived class (if derived classes are allowed) as an actual argument. Some functions have no choice but to accept a reference, for example, the copy constructor. This means that the receiving function must deal with the argument through an interface guaranteed to be preserved in derived classes. This needn't be the public interface; the interface can be public, protected, or even private. However, it must remain a valid interface in all derived classes, or the function call will fail when used with derived classes.

Note that there are two responsibilities here: the base class designer must design an interface for derived classes that allows them to maintain the interface semantics, and clients of a class that permits polymorphism must allow for it.

If you can't make this guarantee, explicitly state in the class' documentation that it can't be used as a public base class.

Implement full protocol in derived classes

If a base class is public, the derived class must correctly implement all aspects of the base class' public interface (or the inherited implementation must operate correctly). Every member function must function properly for the same range of arguments as accepted by the base class. If this isn't the case, the derived class is not a true subtype of the base, which can cause subtle and mysterious errors. If you don't want to implement everything the base class exports, make it a private base class.

Preserve semantics in a derived class

Even worse than not implementing a base class' public interface is subtly changing its meaning. Any public member function of the base class must not have its semantics changed by the derived class, and must accept the same set of arguments. Again, this is the responsibility of both the base class designer (making preservation of the semantics possible) and the derived class designer (honoring those semantics).

Suppose a class TBase has an `operator==` function that takes a `const TBase&` argument; any override of this function by a derived class TDerived must then preserve its semantics. In particular, the TDerived class override must not assume the argument is of type `const Derived&` and downcast it to that type, because that changes the meaning of the member function that is inherited from TBase's public interface. Downcasts are often a warning sign of such design problems.

In this case, it is better to overload `operator==` to accept an argument of type `const Derived&`, and then either reexport the inherited `operator==` or make the operators global for symmetry.

Be especially careful when you have two or more public base classes; make sure that the semantics of all of them are satisfied, particularly if they export the same or similar protocol. In earlier versions of the Taligent Application Environment, for example, MCollectible had a virtual function, IsEqual, that took a `const MCollectible&` argument and returned a Boolean. Derived classes of MCollectible overrode this function to implement the comparison used when those derived classes were inserted into collections. When one of those MCollectible-derived classes and one of its own derived classes wanted to define a comparison differently, and the derived class was inserted into a collection of base class objects, that collection didn't behave properly. Overriding was not the proper mechanism for this function.

The current Taligent approach, based on templates, works better: specify a comparator object. Default comparators are available that use overloaded `operator==`. If TBase and TDerived both need comparison functions, define them as follows:

```
Boolean operator==(const TBase &, const TBase &);
Boolean operator==(const TDerived &, const TDerived &);
```

✅ NOTE   `operator==` can be defined as either a friend or a member function.

Because of the overloading mechanism, the appropriate comparison function is used for the appropriate object. Another solution for a given collection is to use a pointer to a function or member function to define a comparison, rather than assuming a fixed operator. Or, write a custom comparator.

Watch for this problem: it can cause bugs that are extremely difficult to find. It is especially problematic when inheriting from two or more base classes, each of which defines a function with the same name but with different semantics.

Avoid deep nesting in lightweight objects

Whether you use an object or inherit from it, there's a finite cost. The object you use or inherit from must be constructed or destructed every time your object is constructed or destructed. Usually, that means a function call. Make sure that lightweight objects intended to be created or destroyed quickly do not use deeply nested inheritance or many embedded objects with constructors.

MULTIPLE INHERITANCE

Multiple inheritance is a fairly new feature in object-oriented languages, and it is easy to design a confusing class hierarchy that resembles a bowl of spaghetti. Here are some design guidelines useful for managing multiple inheritance.

Classes in the Taligent Application Environment are artificially partitioned into two categories: *base classes* that represent fundamental functional objects (like a car), and *mixin classes* that represent optional functionality (like power steering). To distinguish between the two, base class names begin with *T*, and mixin class names begin with *M* (see "Name conventions" on page 32). To control multiple inheritance:

A class may inherit from *zero or one* base classes, plus *zero or more* mixin classes. If a class does not inherit from a base class, it probably should be a mixin class (though not always, such as if it is at the root of a hierarchy).

A class that inherits from a base class is itself a base class; it can't be a mixin class. Mixin classes can only inherit from other mixin classes.

The net effect of these two guidelines is that base classes form a conventional, tree-structured inheritance hierarchy rather than an arbitrary acyclic graph. This makes the base class hierarchy much easier to understand. Mixins then become add-in *options* that do not fundamentally alter the inheritance hierarchy.

Like all guidelines, these are not meant to be hard and fast rules. You can and should use multiple inheritance in other ways as well if it makes sense. Remember, people are better at understanding regular structures than arbitrary directed acyclic graphs.

Be aware of problems with virtual bases

When using virtual bases, be aware of these multiple inheritance problems (a Taligent engineer must confirm with an architect before using multiple inheritance):

Virtual bases can be confusing and hard to understand: Try to avoid getting into a situation where you have a virtual base; no matter which alternative you choose, programmers tend to have a hard time understanding them.

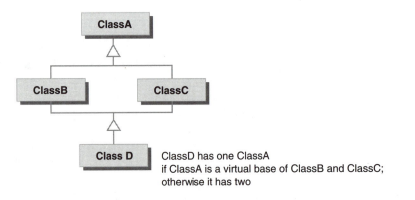

ClassD has one ClassA
if ClassA is a virtual base of ClassB and ClassC;
otherwise it has two

Once you have a pointer to a virtual base, there's no way to convert it back into a pointer to its enclosing class. This means that if you have MCollectible as a virtual base (even indirectly), for example, and stick your object in a collection, there's no way to convert it back to the right type via a cast when you get it out of the collection. This problem doesn't occur with the template versions of the Taligent Collection classes, but watch for it in your own classes. Also, avoid casting base classes to derived classes if at all possible; templates help with that, too.

✅ NOTE   Dynamic casts, a new feature of C++, can circumvent this problem, but are an expensive technique. For information about dynamic casts, see "Avoid type casting" on page 41.

Virtual bases are always initialized by the most derived class, whether they are accessible to that class or not. So, if a class TBase has a private virtual base VVirtual, then constructors for class TDerived (which has TBase as a base) must supply the constructor arguments for VVirtual, even though Virtual is not accessible to TDerived. This is a violation of encapsulation, but that's how it works.

✅ NOTE   A base class should either always be a virtual base or never be a virtual base; it should almost never be a virtual base of some derived classes and a nonvirtual base of others. This is because there are special (and problematic) constructor semantics for virtual base classes that you must take into account in their design. This is also why virtual base classes have special naming conventions. For more information, see "Name conventions" on page 32.

Avoid multiple occurrences of a base

Sometimes the same base class (which should be a mixin) occurs more than once as an ancestor of a class (this often happens with MCollectible). However, only one version of a virtual function can exist for a given class, and it's only useful to have multiple occurrences of a base class if there are data members associated with it.

Although you might need to have the same base class occur more than once, there are costs: there are multiple virtual table pointers and clients who want to cast to the base class that have to supply a casting path to indicate which of the duplicates the cast is for. If you don't need to cast back, and you don't need two copies of the data, this is one of the situations where virtual base classes might be better.

PERFORMANCE BY DESIGN

Good performance is just one attribute of quality code. Like reliability, it comes from two things: designing it in from the beginning and fixing problems with it during debugging.

Design performance in

Designing performance in does not mean writing everything in assembly language. Good micro-level code is only one component of good performance, and it is usually not the most important. *Choosing the right data structures and algorithms* is the most important aspect of getting good performance. Having the fastest linked list code in the world is a waste if you should have used a hash table. Similarly, it isn't smart to use a hash table when all you ever do is sequential access. It is also misspent energy to worry about whether a function call should be inline when the function does a disk operation.

Remember that there is *no* code faster than no code—the best way to speed up code is to eliminate it. If you can avoid a computation by caching the result, or by finding some other way to get what you need, that's a big win.

There's a lot of oral tradition in this area (except that it is written down), and it's well worth reading everything you can get your hands on. Here are some recommended written sources of information on this topic:

- *Writing Efficient Programs* (Bentley).
- "Hints for Computer System Design" (Lampson) in *Proceedings of the Ninth ACM Symposium on Operating System Principles,* Operating System Review Vol. 17 No. 5 (pp. 33–48). Good observations by someone who's been through the wringer a few times.
- *Programming Pearls* and *More Programming Pearls* (Bentley).
- *The Psychology of Computer Programming* (Weinberg) has some choice bits about what drives programmers to worry about efficiency.

Conduct performance analysis

In any complex system (any program longer than three lines), it's not possible to completely determine its behavior *a priori*. To solve performance problems you need hard data. Informed speculation is useful, but your most valuable tool is empiricism. Measure your code to find out what's happening. In addition to the standard performance tools (PC sampling and call tracing), there are some other tricks you can use.

One technique that has worked well in the Taligent Application Environment is to take things out one by one. Set up a timing harness for the code in question; then remove pieces of the computation one by one. This can be very helpful in pinning down where the time is going, something you can't always tell from other techniques. For example, when Taligent engineers worked on the View system, they thought it spent a lot of time in one loop. They put return in front of the loop. The code no longer worked correctly, but it was possible to tell how much time it spent in the loop.

Perform controlled experiments

In the spirit of an empirical approach to performance, make sure you don't change too many variables at once. If you make eight separate changes and then measure a performance difference, you have no idea which changes helped and which hurt.

By making your performance tests controlled experiments, you understand which variables change and which are constant. This lets you know what is effective and what is not.

This doesn't mean you have to make changes one at a time. You can still throw in a whole slew of changes; just make sure you can control them individually. Put each change under the control of a Boolean flag, either local to the object or global to the class. Then you can turn each flag on and off individually or in combination and measure the results.

Use static objects instead of temporaries

One tip for improving performance is to use static objects rather than constant temporaries. Beware of initialization order problems (see "Static object constructors" on page 48 and "Consider alternatives to temporary objects" on page 60).

Use chunky iteration for performance

If you have an iterator over some collection of data, but have performance problems from paying a function call for accessing each member of the collection, you might be tempted to make the internal data structures of that collection public for direct access.

Instead, to preserve data abstraction and still improve performance, amortize the function call over multiple data members, by introducing a *chunky* iterator. A chunky iterator returns multiple data elements at one time. The iterator, not the client, determines the number of elements to return based on the internal structure of the data collection, which the client knows nothing about. The iterator also indicates how many elements were returned with each call.

For example, consider an iterator over a string of characters. Making a function call for each character is very expensive. But exporting the data structure directly precludes using some other data structure in the future. By using a chunky iterator, you can get the best performance possible:

Where the string is just an array of characters, the chunky iterator returns a pointer to the array and the length of the array, thus returning the whole string at once.

For a string that consists of several such arrays (such as text stored in a recursive run array or other noncontiguous chunks), the iterator returns each array successively, indicating how many characters are in each one.

If a string does not use an array of characters internally at all, the iterator has an internal array of characters of some predetermined size (large enough to amortize the costs of the iterator function calls). For each iteration, it copies characters out of the string into its internal array, then returns a pointer to the array and indicates the number of characters.

In each case, the client knows nothing about the internal data structures, and still gets good performance. It's even possible to preserve the easier *one-at-a-time* interface by using inline functions that turn around and call the chunky interface (in fact, it is preferable because it is simpler for clients). This is the technique used by TStream and the C `stdio` library functions, such as `getchar()`.

Use cache objects

Creating and destroying objects can take a lot of time. If you can, consider holding onto objects for longer periods and reusing them. This makes the most sense for heavyweight objects: lighter ones can be cheaper to create than the caching mechanism. In addition, watch out for concurrency issues you might not have with locally created objects but that might show up with a cache.

COMMON DESIGN PROBLEMS AND PITFALLS

Object-oriented design is an iterative process. Don't be afraid to change your class design based on experience you gain, and don't be afraid to change it for a second, third, or fourth time. You will be rewarded by seeing layers of cruft drop out of your code. If the class design isn't right, the grief that clients might have down the road will overshadow the inconvenience of having changed the design up front. Fix design problems as early as possible; redesigning late in the development cycle is always a problem (and often impossible).

Design is as much about discovery as it is about construction.

Object bloat

Object bloat (TKitchenSink) is a symptom of failure to reconsider your design (see "Hardening of the architecture" on page 23). A class definition starts out simple and clean, but as time goes on and changes are made, it becomes larger and larger, with the class *identity* becoming harder to state concisely. Some of the possible actions to solve this problem are:

- Move some of the functions into new classes that the object would use.
- Break up the class into two or more classes.
- Rethink the class definition based on experience gained.

This isn't an exhaustive list. A rule of thumb is: if you can't give a concise human language definition of the class, you likely have a problem.

Lost object focus

Lost object focus is another manifestation of problems with class definitions. An object's purpose is stated in its class definition (remember, the class definition is more than just the C++ declaration). A class might start with a concise definition, but over time the definition becomes fuzzy or nonexistent. You might also have a reasonable class definition, but one function might not fit in with the rest.

The only solution to this problem is the same as for object bloat: keep a careful eye on the class design and make sure that an object's role remains well defined. If an object loses focus, you need to modify the design.

No complex software system winds up with the same design it started with.

This is terribly important. The ability to easily work with any object-oriented system depends on how well the classes are defined. If the classes are clearly delineated, well defined, and self-contained, a developer can treat them as abstractions. The less this is true, the more the developer must treat them as collections of loosely related functions, which increases the complexity. People deal with complexity by inventing abstractions. To help them, make sure that:

- The abstractions exist.
- You supply abstractions so that developers do not need to invent their own.
- Your classes map onto the abstractions directly.

Hardening of the architecture

Hardening of the architecture happens when you keep making incremental changes to an existing class. If it doesn't quite handle a situation, someone adds a tweak. When the next problem comes up, another tweak is added. Or when a new feature is requested, another tweak is added, and so on.

One of the most important skills you can develop is a little red warning light inside your head that causes you to think, "Wait a minute, this is starting to get messy." When your class gets convoluted, it's time to reexamine the design. Here are some of the warning signs that the time has arrived:

There are bugs because the internal state of an object is too hard to track and fixes consist of adding patches. Patches are characterized by code that looks like: "If this is the case, then force that to be true," or "Do this just in case we need to," or "Do this before calling that function, because it expects this."

There are member functions that do not fit in very well with the class definition. (See "Object bloat" and "Lost object focus" on page 22.)

If you can't tell whether or not code is needed, your design is getting out of control.

Structification

Structification results in an implementation and interface that are closely related; the interface merely parrots the internal implementation of the class. The result is almost never a good class definition. Structification is a technique for class creation that results from the following sequence of events:

1. You have a `struct`.

2. You replace `struct` with `class`.

3. You make all data members `private`.

4. For every data member foo, you define GetFoo and SetFoo.

Get and set functions are a natural part of a well-designed interface, but an interface that is long on state-related functions and short on members that actually perform an action is a sign of a bad design. Avoid it.

Modulitis

Modulitis occurs when you take a C header file (or Pascal unit), make it a class, and turn all functions into members. A good way to recognize this problem is when member functions do not refer to the `this` pointer, either directly or indirectly, or when the class has nothing but static members. The result is usually a poor class definition.

Managers are not objects

The presence of a manager object typically signifies a problem with your design, the result of which is a client interface expressed as objects outside the client's problem domain. The word *manager* in a class name often indicates this problem. A centralized implementation, either within an address space or between address spaces, is just an implementation detail. For example, suppose you want a function to apply to multiple windows, such as CloseAllOpenWindows. The wrong way to do this is to have clients call a TWindowManager class. The correct way is to make CloseAllOpenWindows a static member of TWindow. It is associated with the class it applies to, and its multiobject function is reflected by its being static.

Class definitions reflect the important objects from the client's problem domain, not from the programmer's implementation domain.

Collections of functions are not objects

A manifestation of modulitis is collecting associated functions into an object. Functions must live with the objects that they affect, not in handy packages. Functions that apply to more than one object usually should be static members. Only when you apply overloading (as in the case of operators, or with some templates) is it appropriate to use true global functions—that is, those outside the scope of any class.

Encapsulation leakage

This problem occurs when details about a class' internal implementation start to leak out through the interface. As more internal details become visible, there is less flexibility to make changes in the future. If an implementation is completely open, there is almost no flexibility for future changes.

It is fine to reveal implementation when it's intentional, necessary, and carefully controlled. However, don't make such a decision lightly: it is quite easy to do it by accident.

For example, public or protected data members or inline functions that access private data members reveal an important aspect of your implementation. If developers use those functions (not just application developers, but any programmer building on top of the Taligent Application Environment), the system's requirement of binary compatibility means that you can't:

- Change the location or type of that data member in your class.
- Change the semantics of the member, control how its contents are changed, or control when they can be changed.

Also watch out for member functions that return a reference or pointer to a data member of the object. Although this gives you the flexibility of moving that data member around, it is equivalent to declaring the member public and should be avoided. More controlled versions of the same thing return a const pointer (at least the caller can't change the member) or have a pair of member functions along the lines of "I want to *use* this subobject" and "I'm *done with* this subobject."

This latter variety is especially desirable because it gives you the flexibility to synthesize the object on request. If the functions are the constructor or destructor of an *accessor* object, you can let C++ handle exceptions for you (see "Exception handling" on page 74).

It is also possible to achieve the efficiency of pointers while retaining copying semantics (see "Surrogate objects" on page 91).

Empty base classes

An empty base class occurs when an abstract base class has no member functions other than the constructor and destructor (or other special members). Many developers create such base classes because there is some idea they want to have represented by a class, even though it has no protocol.

Base classes (especially public ones) should exist only if there is protocol to be inherited. Public bases should only exist if they are to be used polymorphically. If there is no such protocol, there is no type relationship (or behavior inheritance), and there is no need for a base class. If you wind up in this situation, rethink your class hierarchy. Not every idea needs to be expressed as a class, and classes don't always correspond one-to-one with real-world entities.

Overeducated base classes

The opposite of the empty base class is a base class that contains members that aren't meaningful for all of its derived classes. The correct design solution is to push those members down into a derived class—either a concrete class or a less abstract base class. For example, originally the Video Device framework had protocol in the TVideoDevice base class for setting pixel depths, loading color tables, and so on. These operations pertain only to frame buffers, and not all video devices are necessarily frame buffers (such as intelligent graphics boards).

Overachieving base classes

Avoid functionality in base classes that all derived classes will not use, especially if they have to override it to turn it off. An exception is *default* implementations that work for most derived classes and are intended to be overridden.

**Distinguish is-a
from has-a
relationships**

Failure to correctly distinguish between is-a and has-a relationships is a common design problem. It happens most often when a class should be a member, or a private base class is inherited as a public base class.

Use public base classes only when polymorphism is important, and the derived class is used through a pointer or reference to the base class.

Use a private or protected base when behavior is going to be inherited: polymorphism is not needed, but you want to use the class as a base internally, or the base will be called from within a framework. This is like public inheritance, but only visible to your own class or to a framework.

Use a member when behavior is only going to be used, and when your class is a client of that behavior.

CHAPTER 3

C++ PROGRAMMING CONVENTIONS

A software engineer's responsibility is to produce a business asset that is going to last many years. If an engineer can't understand someone else's code, it might as well be thrown away and rewritten from scratch. Unfortunately this happens all too often. Making code readable and maintainable is as important as, or more important than, making it work correctly. If it doesn't work, it can be fixed. If it can't be maintained, it's scrap.

THE C++ STANDARD

History shows that designing language extensions is a nontrivial exercise, especially with a complex language like C++. The trail of the C++ standardization effort is littered with innocuous-looking extensions that proved to be extremely difficult to define in a rigorous fashion. Trying to define and implement nonstandard features can be very difficult and time consuming, so if you are on a project team trying to ship a product in a short time, avoid nonstandard extensions. Taligent C++ code doesn't assume anything more than what is defined by the current ISO/ANSI C++ draft standard.

✔ NOTE   A runtime can be extended because it's implemented by a runtime library, not by the compiler. For example, the capabilities of Taligent's runtime that Taligent's C++ code depends on (such as dynamic class loading) can be emulated by the runtimes of most C++ systems.

At Taligent, use of language constructs or implementation dependencies beyond those specified by the ISO/ANSI C++ draft standard must be approved by the architecture team. No such additions have been approved for the Taligent Application Environment beyond dynamic class loading.

SOURCE FILE CONVENTIONS

Source file conventions are the basic rules for managing and documenting source files when programming in C++.

Include copyright notices

If your system doesn't support the "©" character, make sure that you spell out "Copyright"

No publication in 1993

To assist in protecting your organization's intellectual property, include a copyright notice at the front of every file you create:

```
// Copyright © 1994 YourCompany, Inc. All rights reserved.
```

If you significantly modify a file, list the year of the modification. The years correspond to publication, not creation, dates. Separate consecutive years with a dash, but off-years with a comma.

```
// Copyright © 1992, 1994-1996 Taligent, Inc. All rights reserved.
```

Any binary files you ship should contain, within the first fifty lines, a copyright notice that appears if the code is displayed or printed.

Use comments

Comments aren't a replacement for reading the code; source code should be as readable as possible. However, the source code isn't capable of representing all information concerning a subtle implementation. If source code isn't *completely obvious*, include a comment.

Comments complement source code; they don't parrot it.

Make comments short and informative, and echo the code as little as possible. As a rule of thumb, if you must read the code a couple of times to figure out what is happening, include a comment.

Include function prototypes

Omit dummy parameter names in function declarations only if the meaning is clear without them. It's almost always necessary to include parameter names when you have more than one parameter of the same type; otherwise it's impossible to figure out which one is which.

If you are getting compiler warnings such as "warning: foo not used" where foo is a parameter of a function, stop the warning by leaving the parameter name out of the function header for the function's *definition* (you can include the parameter name inside a /* */ comment). Whether or not a parameter name appears in the function's declaration has no bearing on the warning.

Do not use code names in filenames

Code names change all too frequently and are easily misunderstood when encountered at a later date, such as by another developer trying to maintain your code. Therefore, the names of files should never contain code names. (This is also true for names within header and source files.) Always use straightforward, meaningful names. See "Name conventions" on page 32 for more information.

Enclose definitions in header files

Enclose all header file definitions, and all the necessary antecedents, in a #ifndef construct. This saves you and your clients from having to figure out whether you have already included them.

Enclose definitions in a #ifndef construct

The symbol is your company's name, followed by one underline, followed by the filename in uppercase (without the .h)

```
// MyClass.h
#ifndef Taligent_MYCLASS
#define Taligent_MYCLASS
#ifndef Taligent_PREREQUISITE1
#include "prerequisite1.h"
#endif
#ifndef Taligent_PREREQUISITE2
#include "prerequisite2.h"
#endif
... definitions for MyClass
#endif
```

Now developers can include your header as many times as they want without errors. More importantly, you can include your header's prerequisites without caring whether they've already been included elsewhere (assuming that everyone follows this convention).

To speed up compilation, use the following construct in your files that include other files. (Don't use this for ANSI C or C++ header files because the symbols vary between compilers.):

```
#ifndef MyCompany_FOO
#include "Foo.h"
#endif
```

This skips the overhead of reading and parsing Foo.h. This practice works especially well with symbol table load/dump; because the dump file defines the symbols, the include files need not be opened at all.

**Include only
related classes
in one file**

To keep your class definitions under control and to make life easier for those trying to decipher them, limit each header file to a single class definition or a set of related class definitions. This is a common convention, and a compiler with a load/dump facility removes the penalty for having many small include files rather than a few large ones.

Put only one class implementation in a given source file; declare and implement classes private to the class implementation in the same source file. Name the file after the class, but without the initial *T*. For example, put the class TContainerView in `ContainerView.C`. Also, be consistent about case when naming and referring to include files, as some development environments are sensitive to case in filenames.

NAME CONVENTIONS

Select C++ identifiers (including types, functions, and classes) carefully. When a programmer sees a name, it might be out of context; choose names to enhance readability and comprehension. A name that seems cute or easy to type can cause trouble to someone trying to decipher code. Remember, code is read many more times than it is written; err on the side of long, readable names. Internal code names should not appear anywhere in the interfaces to the system. Even inside your implementation, it's better to use the prosaic form if there is one.

To make the scope of names explicit, Taligent uses the following conventions.

Name conventions

Identifier	Convention	Example
Types	Begin with a capital letter	Boolean
Base classes	Begin with *T*	TContainerView
Mixin classes	Begin with *M*; see "Multiple inheritance" on page 17	MPrintable
Enumeration types	Begin with *E*	EFreezeLevel
Raw C types	Avoid using C types; see "Avoid raw C types with dimensions" on page 40	
Virtual base classes	Begin with *V,* rather than *T* or *M*	VBaseClass
Members	Begin with *f* for *field*[1]; functions begin with a capital letter	fViewList, DrawSelf()
Static variables	Begin with *g*; applies to static variables in functions and global variables (excluding static data members of a class)	gDeviceList
Static data members	Begin with *fg*; includes class globals	TView::fgTokenClient
Locals and parameters	Begin with a word whose initial letter is lowercase; local automatic variables only, treat statics like globals	seed, port, theCurrentArea
Constants	Begin with *k*; including names of enumeration constants and constant statics	kMenuCommand
Acronyms	All uppercase	TNBPName, not TNbpName
Template arguments	Begin with *A*	AType
Getters and setters	Begin with *Set...*, *Get...*, or *Is...* (Boolean); use sparingly (see "Structification" on page 23)	SetLast(), GetNext(), IsDone()
Allocator and adopters	Begin with *Create...*, *Copy...*, *Adopt...*, or *Orphan...*; see "Use special names for copy, create, and adopt routines" on page 35	CreateName()

[1] *Field* is a historical name for data member

In any name that contains more than one word, the first word follows the convention for the type of the name, and subsequent words follow with the first letter of each word capitalized, such as TTextBase. Do not use underscores except for #define symbols.

Use specific names

In general, make names specific rather than generic. For example, the type for Taligent's graphics coordinates was once called Number; out of context, this is very hard to figure out and likely to accidentally conflict with identifiers from other header files. The new type, GCoordinate, is far more descriptive. Use generic names only when there is true generality, such as TSetOf.

But use generic names for abstract base classes

The most abstract base class in a hierarchy should have the most generic, abstract name, with names of subclasses denoting refinement. Don't give an abstract base class a name that is derived from a concrete derived class. Also, avoid names like TBaseFoo or TAbstractFoo, where TFoo is a subclass, because nothing in the name distinguishes TFoo from other subclasses of TBaseFoo. TStandardFoo is only marginally better, but acceptable.

✓ NOTE   There is an exception: if your abstract base class can have one and only one concrete derived class, it is acceptable to give that derived class the generic name. In that case, the abstract class should have *Abstract* in its name. For example, the model class hierarchy has TAbstractModel, from which descended TModel and TModelSurrogate. TModel is the base for all concrete derived classes (as a surrogate, TModelSurrogate doesn't count).

If you find you have trouble with these rules, perhaps your class hierarchy needs rethinking. For example, an earlier text class hierarchy included TText and TBaseText; TBaseText was an abstract base class from which TText descends. Normally, TText, as the more generic name, should be used for the base class. The new hierarchy works this way, with TStandardText as the default implementation.

Avoid abbreviations

Avoid abbreviations whenever possible, especially ad hoc ones. If you use commonly or easily understood abbreviations, use them consistently. Inconsistent abbreviations make it difficult to remember the correct name of a function or variable, as for example, using VisibleRegion some places and VisRgn others. Remember, code is read many more times than it is written: long, readable names will better stand the test of time.

Use special names for copy, create, and adopt routines

Routines that allocate, manage, or take responsibility for storage have special names and abide by the following guidelines:

Routines that make a new object that the caller must delete begin with *Create...*

Routines that copy an existing object, where the caller must delete the copy, begin with *Copy...* A member function that copies an object should be *Copy()*.

Routines that abandon an object and pass deletion responsibility to the caller begin with *Orphan...*

Routines that accept an object the caller has allocated and take responsibility for eventually deleting it begin with *Adopt...* (This style of programming is error prone; avoid it if possible.)

Adopting routines that cannot follow the previous rule (such as constructors) start the name of the argument with *adopt...*

Use global names only for classes

Ideally, only classes should have names with global scope (that is, not nested within a class). For this reason, avoid globally scoped functions, enumeration types, or constants. Make functions static members of some class, and define enums and constants within a class. It's even possible to nest classes inside other classes, if they don't need global scope. There are only two general exceptions; (at Taligent, an architect must approve all others):

- Functions (such as operators) that must be declared as friends rather than members.
- Some template functions.

By keeping the global name space uncluttered, you reduce name collisions and make it easier to figure out where a name is coming from. C++ helps by allowing declarations in class scope, allowing static members, and providing qualification to access identifiers declared inside classes.

```
class TFoo {
public:
    enum EWho {kFred, kBarney};
...
};

TFoo::EWho person = TFoo::kFred;
```

This lets you put constants associated with different classes into different name spaces, similar to when C changed a few years back so that structure members from different struct's were in different name spaces.

🌀 NOTE   All nested declarations appear in the class' name space, even the enumeration type. Because class declarations can be nested, scopes can nest to multiple levels and require multiple levels of qualification. Within the body of a class, however, names declared in its scope don't require qualification.

To avoid name collisions, use static members to put ordinary functions and global variables into the scope of their associated class.

Place ordinary functions and global variables into the scope of their associated class

```
class TView {
public:
    static void Initialize();
    static const TText kMagicWord;
    static const long kMagicNumber;
...
};

TView::Initialize();
...TView::kMagicWord...
i = TView::kMagicNumber;
```

Avoid ordinary globals

Most global functions and variables should be static members of some class. The same applies to constants—make them members of an enumeration inside a class, if possible. Global variables that aren't constants of the sort illustrated in the previous example shouldn't be public at all; instead, access them through member functions, static or normal:

```
class TFoo {
public:
    static Boolean fgSomeFlag;       // BAD!
}

TFoo::fgSomeFlag = TRUE;             // BAD!
```

The C++ namespace feature allows the same kind of scoping control for global names. A namespace construct acts like a class definition by providing a name scope. Unlike class declarations, declarations within a name space needn't be contiguous—for example, declarations in the same name space can be in different header files. Also, there is a *using* construct that imports names from a name space into the local scope. The Taligent Application Environment might use the namespace feature; however, it is better to move names into class scope.

CLASS DEFINITION CONVENTIONS

When the MacApp® application framework was being created, issues arose regarding conventions such as how to indicate certain attributes of member functions, and whether they are called by clients never, rarely, or often. Based on experience with the MacApp software, such conventions do not sufficiently express the information a client or derived class needs. However, there are a few conventions that help.

It's much better to spell things out explicitly than to expect people to infer them from the declaration.

Follow member function conventions

Follow these conventions when designing and using member functions:

Protected constructors or pure virtual functions indicate an abstract base class in the Taligent Application Environment (in C++, only a pure virtual function indicates an abstract base class; protected constructors do not).

A private copy constructor or assignment operator indicates a class that cannot be copied.

A function whose implementation is inline doesn't change its implementation (although it might be extended).

Protected members can only be accessed by derived classes.

Private virtual functions can be overridden but not called.

If a member function is defined to have no implementation (for all eternity), it is permissible to define it as an empty body in the class declaration. This is much better than not providing a constructor at all.

```
class TFoo {
public:
    TFoo() {};          // Will ALWAYS be empty!
};
```

✓ NOTE   Don't assume that a virtual function may be overridden. The class author might want to allow overriding in the future, but that doesn't mean you may override it now. The rules for subclassing must be spelled out in the class' documentation (see "Design the interfaces between the base and derived classes" on page 14). *Never* override a function that isn't documented to be overridable. And *never* override a function in a way that isn't in accordance with its documentation.

In general, define an empty body only for special members of abstract base classes with no implementation or storage.

State explicit use of public, private, and protected

Though C++ frequently allows you to leave out the private keyword, don't do it. Class definitions should always explicitly state the visibility of their members and base classes. When you have multiple instances of the sections, they should appear in the following order (such as one set of public-protected-private followed by another set of public-protected-private):

```
class TFoo: public TBar, protected MBlat, private MBaz {
public:
    // public members;

protected:
    // protected members;

private:
    // private members;
};
```

Always state public sections first and private sections last. You may omit any section

✔ NOTE   The private section is necessary only to make the compiler happy, so it should be last. When using the Taligent Development System, the private interface might not even be visible to clients, and the protected interface might only be visible to subclasses (private virtual functions are an exception).

Use separate class definition sections

Frequently you have functions that must be public, but that are not meant to be called by clients. Consider a function that is called only by another related class which you don't want to make a friend. To clarify the use of these members, separate them in the class declaration into sections according to who usually calls them, with a comment at the front of each section. Place private virtual member functions that are meant to be overridden ahead of public functions that clients and subclasses should not call.

```
class TFoo {
public:

    // Normal client functions:
    void Member1();
    ...

    // Seldom-used functions:
    void BlueMoon1();

protected:
    ...

public:
    // Internal use only; do not call:
    void MagicMember1();

private:
    ...
};
```

Group functions in sections according to who

A separate public section just before the private section for functions not called by clients

Public and internal aren't the only categories into which members fall: feel free to divide them up into as many sections as you like to help people to understand them, for example, API, SPI, and internal.

✓ NOTE   If the set of users of internal public members is small, fixed, and known, use the C++ `friend` feature and make them private instead. This gives you more control (see "Friend functions and classes" on page 74).

TYPE DECLARATION CONVENTIONS

One way to think of types is as if they were physical units, like kilograms or watts or furlongs per fortnight. These are all distinct types, and trying to mix them is like mixing apples and oranges. When making a declaration, think about whether you should use an existing type or make a new type to distinguish a new usage.

Avoid raw C types with dimensions

Declare types rather than using raw C types so that if your implementation changes, you don't have to do a lot of editing by hand. It's much better to declare a type (via `class` definition or `typedef`) that represents the abstract concept, and to phrase your declarations that way. This lets you change your implementation by editing the original type definition.

Instead of...

```
long time;
short mouseX;
char *menuName;
```

Use (for example)

```
typedef long TimeStamp;
typedef short Coordinate;
class TString { ... };

...

TimeStamp time;
Coordinate mouseX
TString menuName;
```

✅ NOTE   A `typedef` doesn't introduce a new, distinct type; it's just a synonym. Also, the compiler doesn't warn you if you mix it with any other type that is defined synonymously.

For more information about raw C types, see "Bad assumptions" on page 110.

Use dimensionless raw C types

It's acceptable to use a raw C type under certain circumstances, such as when the quantity is machine dependent, or when it can be characterized as a dimensionless number (for example, a small int). Otherwise, it's best to give yourself flexibility.

However, types that merely wrap existing C types are not helpful:

```
typedef unsigned char UChar;        // Bad usage
```

Either use a raw C type because it's a dimensionless number and falls within the definition of the C type, or define a typedef based on the *function* of the type, not its concrete representation. To help you with this, the header file PrimitiveTypes.h contains useful definitions of primitive types. Two ANSI C header files, stddef.h and limits.h, contain definitions as well, here are two:

size_t   The type returned by the built-in C sizeof function. This is useful for
                  representing the sizes of things.

ptrdiff_t   A type that can represent the difference between any two pointers.

You might have noticed that these names don't conform to Taligent conventions. In the interest of clarity and portability, it is better to use the names as defined by ISO/ANSI C. However, a useful non-ISO/ANSI C type is void*, which is for pointers to raw storage.

✅ NOTE   If a data type is unsigned, declare it unsigned; this helps avoid nasty bugs down the road.

Avoid type casting

Type casting, though dangerous and very uncontrolled, is occasionally necessary in C and C++; however, always question the need before you use it. There are three kinds of casts in C++:

A cast can change an object from one type to another. This includes casts between the built-in arithmetic types, and casts involving classes (not pointers to classes) or pointers to classes related by inheritance. These are fairly safe, because an actual *conversion* is taking place.

A cast that involves pointers and type *coercion*. This is the killer. The bit pattern of one type is interpreted as another type. This is very unsafe, and causes your code to die horribly (or worse, die subtly).

A runtime-checked cast takes the form dynamic_cast<type>(expression). At run time, if the type of the expression can be converted to *type*, you get that type; otherwise, you get 0 or an exception. Although this type of conversion is safe and can be very handy (for more dynamic dispatching and for optimizations), it is easy to abuse. Talk to your architect before using it.

Silent coercion

Unfortunately, some C++ constructs can be interpreted as either conversion or coercion. For example, a cast from one class pointer type to another is *conversion* if the two types are related by type inheritance, but *coercion* if they are not. The C++ compiler doesn't necessarily warn you if you intend the former but wind up with the latter. Worse still, a cast between pointers to member functions can be a conversion for the class, but a coercion for the function prototype.

Some types of casts are always coercion—for instance, casting a `const` or volatile pointer to one without those same attributes. If you make a member function `const` because it doesn't change the object semantics, you must cast your `this` pointer to non-`const` to make changes to the internal object state (unless your compiler supports `mutable`). Avoid this technique. Instead, overload the function or try another way (see "Concurrency and shared library issues" on page 99).

Casts to and from `void*` are dangerous, but in a fairly local way. Avoid such casts except where necessary. Do *not* use `void*` to avoid specifying a type for a variable or parameter. Use it only for manipulation of raw storage. (See "Avoid storage manipulation in open code" on page 98 for information about raw storage.)

Finally, although casts from a base class pointer to a derived class pointer are conversions (known as *type narrowing*), avoid them. If you accidentally specify types not related by inheritance, you silently get a coercion. This is also a poor programming technique and removes important information used for type checking. Templates in C++ and the Taligent Collection classes obviate the need for most such casts.

Cast operators

C++ now has a set of operators for performing casts. These operators remove the risk of unintended consequences for casting by making the programmer's intention explicit. However, they still don't make casting a good approach to a design. Very few compilers currently support these operators, but as they become widely available, use them as a safer alternative to old-style casts:

`static_cast<target_type>(expression)` performs a conversion from the type of the expression to the target type, if such a conversion is allowed. It never silently reinterprets bits as a different type.

`const_cast<target_type>(expression)` removes `const` and `volatile` modifiers. The target type must be the same as the type of the expression, except for `const` or `volatile` modifiers.

`reinterpret_cast<target_type>(expression)` coerces the expression to be the target type, without conversion. This is inherently unsafe and implementation dependent.

Summary

- The only generally acceptable casts are the conversion type.
- Avoid all casts involving pointers unless absolutely necessary.
- Nonpointer casts can never silently become coercions.

For a complete description of the casting operators, see an up-to-date C++ language reference.

Use consistent return types for assignment operators

Assignment operators should return a type that is consistent to the client. Usually this is a non-`const` reference, because that is what the built-in types and the standard C++ library classes return. Declare assignment operators like this:

```
class TFoo {
    ...
    TFoo& operator=(argument);      // "argument" is usually: const TFoo &
```

State `typedef` class names before specifications

When declaring a `typedef` of `class`, place the name between the data type and the member specifications.

Correct form ──────

```
typedef class T {...};
```

For compatibility with C, many compilers currently support declaring the name after the member specifications, though this is bad form and not guaranteed to be supported by C++ compilers.

Bad form ────────────

```
typedef class {...} T;
```

> ✅ NOTE   A C++ *class*-type is a `class`, `struct`, or `union`.

ARGUMENTS AND FUNCTION RESULTS

Use the following conventions for function arguments and function results (at Taligent, any deviation requires an architect's approval). Additionally, for information about when to pass a reference as opposed to a pointer, see "Use references for a one-time reference" on page 46.

Here are some rules for what a function should return:

Return results by value only when there is no need for polymorphism and when the size of the type isn't too large, because the result will be copied. Remember, if you return an object by value, one of its constructors will be called (see the ISO/ANSI C++ draft standard for details on function result semantics).

Use a pointer to return an alias from a function. If storage is being allocated on behalf of the caller, the function name should start with *Create...* or *Copy...* (see "Name conventions" on page 32).

Never return references from functions (or at least check with your architect first). It isn't possible to bound the reference's scope of use (unlike when a reference is passed in, in which case it is guaranteed not to be used after the function call). If you must do this, return a pointer (but see "Avoid returning pointers without allocation" on page 45).

Pass variables when possible

When polymorphism is possible, allow the caller to pass in a variable (via reference) for the result of a function rather than creating and returning a result yourself. For example, if you make a call that returns a collection of things, it is better to let the caller specify the kind of the collection (by supplying it) rather than creating a collection and passing it back. By specifying the argument type as TCollectionOf<> & (or a subclass, if you need to be more restrictive), you give the caller flexibility to choose the appropriate collection type. It also eliminates a potential source of storage leaks. However, beware of assignment to these parameters: unless the assignment operator is virtual, such assignments might slice.

Use array arguments instead of pointers

Use [] instead of * for arrays in argument lists, because it is clearer.

Limit default arguments

Default arguments are a C++ feature that let you avoid overloading functions in some circumstances. Although they are OK to use, they have several properties that restrict their use.

Avoid more than one or two default arguments. If you have that many options on a function or constructor, rethink your interface. Specifying large numbers of options via function arguments is confusing and not very extensible. *Having* large numbers of options is also confusing.

Default arguments constitute a form of inline declaration. Specifically, a declaration with default arguments like this

```
class TFoo {
public:
    void Bar(int iItem = 10);
};
```

is exactly equivalent to the following inline declaration, with all of the consequences that implies (see "Inline functions" on page 62):

```
class TFoo {
public:
    void Bar(int iItem);
    inline void Bar() { Bar(10); };
};
```

If you ever want to change the value of the default argument, or if it might ever become convenient to specifically handle the case with no argument, you don't have that option; the call to Bar(int iItem) with a value of 10 is compiled directly into client code. There's no way to go back and make it call Bar() instead.

If you ever want the option of changing what happens, use overloading instead of default arguments.

Avoid functions with unspecified arguments (...)

C++ allows you to declare functions that take unspecified numbers and types of arguments. The classic example is:

```
void printf(char *, ...);
```

This leftover feature from C subverts quality programming. There are very few functions that need an interface like this; use default arguments or function overloading instead.

Avoid returning pointers without allocation

When you return an internal pointer to an internal object, you reveal the object's existence. Consider what this revelation will cost you in the future. It doesn't matter whether the object is a direct member of the called object, or whether it is allocated and pointed to by the called object. If you return a pointer from a function and you're not allocating memory, and if the pointer points to an independent object that is already visible to the caller, there is no problem. (Although in any open network of data structures you must think carefully about memory management, concurrency, and so on—but that's another problem.)

If you simply return an internal pointer, you must consider that the caller can retain and use this pointer for an arbitrarily long time.

- Be sure to specify how long the pointer is good for—don't assume the developer realizes it's no good after you delete the object that returned it.
- Specify what the caller can do with the returned pointer, especially if it isn't const—the caller can modify the object (though the latter possibility isn't acceptable at Taligent).
- If the caller can modify the pointee at any time (in another thread, asynchronously!?) you will have a hard time figuring out how to use it within your class.

A better approach is to bound the use of the subobject by requiring callers to declare when they are done with it. For example, imagine member functions (like UseObject) that return a modifiable pointer to the subobject, and those that (like DoneWithObject)invalidate that pointer and give the container a chance to react to any changes. This approach is also good for const pointers, as it gives you a chance to synthesize the subobject if you don't want it around all the time (you can delete the synthesized object at the DoneWithObject call). Of course, this only works for one client at a time.

Even better is to use the lifetime of a lightweight object to bound the access to the subobject, rather than explicit UseObject and DoneWithObject calls.

The best approach is not to return pointers to subobjects. Instead, use lightweight surrogate objects to set and get subobjects by value, and to obviate the need for pointers. This technique also works with concurrency. For more on this technique, see "Surrogate objects" on page 91.

REFERENCE AND VALUE SEMANTICS: C++ VERSUS EVERYTHING ELSE

C++ treats pointers differently than other object-based languages, such as Object Pascal or Smalltalk. C++ is value based and treats classes like primitive types, whereas Object Pascal and Smalltalk are reference based (assignment means copying a pointer) and treat objects very differently from primitive types. This is a benefit of C++, because it handles all types in the same style, as opposed to multiple styles in Object Pascal (Smalltalk, like C++, is also self-consistent). However, there are some implications for your C++ programming style.

Use pointers to make multiple references

Use pointers when you want multiple references (aliases) to the same object or a dynamic data structure. If you really just want to pass something by reference to avoid copying, use a reference instead. In fact, pass a class by value if the copying overhead isn't too high and you don't care about polymorphism (for example, if the class has no virtual functions).

Use references for a one-time reference

C++ provides two mechanisms for accessing objects indirectly: pointers and references. By using pointers and references appropriately, you can increase the readability of your code by giving the reader hints as to what is going on. These mechanisms have a lot in common (indeed, they are implemented the same way), so it is important to know which one to use and when.

Use references when a parameter is to be passed *by reference*; the called function forgets about the argument as soon as it returns. Use a regular reference if you are going to modify the argument (TFoo&), and a const reference if you aren't going to modify it but don't want the overhead of call by value (const TFoo&).

Use pointers when the function you call retains a reference (an *alias*) to the object you are passing in, such as when you construct a dynamic data structure. For example, when you put an object into one of the Taligent Collection classes, the collection retains a pointer to your object. Explicitly using pointers lets the reader know that aliasing is occurring.

Developers sometimes pass in a nil pointer to indicate a default value. The correct way to achieve the same effect is to provide a reference with a static default argument, or to overload the function:

```
class TFoo {
public:
    static const TBar kDefault;

    Technique1(const TBar &arg = kDefault);

    Technique2(const TBar &arg);
    Technique2();
};
```

Allocate storage only if you must

Leave storage allocation up to the class client. In a reference-based language like Object Pascal or Smalltalk, all objects are allocated on the heap. In C++, it's better to treat values the same way you would in C. For example, overload the assignment operator instead of defining a copy function; have the caller pass one in by reference and set it instead of allocating and returning an object. This allows you to treat classes just like primitive types, and in the same style.

By doing so, you can make use of one of C++'s unique features: the ability to have automatic and static objects, and objects as members of classes. No matter how clever or efficient the storage allocator, it can never be as fast as allocating an object on the stack, or as part of another object. If an object can be local to a function, there is no storage allocation overhead. Many objects have very localized scope and do not need to be allocated on the heap.

✅ NOTE   There is one exception to the rule about allocating an object and returning a pointer: you must do this when the type of the returned object might vary. A Taligent example is TCollectionOf, which has the virtual function CreateIterator, that returns an iterator for the collection. This is done because different subclasses of TCollectionOf return different subclasses of TIteratorOver. You can't tell until run time what subclass of TCollectionOf you have, so you can't preallocate the iterator; the CreateIterator function must allocate it for you and return it. Any time a function must choose what type of object to return, the function must allocate the object, not the caller.

✅ NOTE   It is useful to allow for monomorphic allocation when it's permitted. For example, if you know the type of a collection, you can declare the iterator yourself rather than call CreateIterator.

It is still appropriate for the caller to allocate storage even when the type of the object being passed in might vary, because you can use references, like pointers, polymorphically (that is, you can specify a TSubFoo& to an argument of type TFoo&). The key question is whether the caller or the function must determine the type. In the former case, leave allocation to the client; in the latter, the function must allocate the object on the heap and return it.

Pretend everything is a primitive

Design your classes so that using them is just like using a primitive type in C. This allows the client to use them in a style which is natural for C. In cases where you want to avoid copying, pass arguments by reference. Use pointers only when you want a truly dynamic data structure, or when polymorphism demands it (note that references allow for polymorphism also, as they are really just a different kind of pointer).

If your problem naturally calls for value semantics, but you don't want to pay the overhead of copying, see "Surrogate objects" on page 91.

STATIC OBJECT CONSTRUCTORS

Don't rely on static objects in other files being available in functions called at static constructor time. C++ guarantees that, within a file, static objects are constructed in order from the top of the file to the bottom. But the order of execution isn't guaranteed between files. If, in the course of executing the constructor for a static object, you make reference to another static object (directly or indirectly, through a function call), the chances are 50-50 that the other static object's constructor hasn't executed yet, and the reference will fail.

It's not clear that this problem can be overcome, especially in the context of shared libraries. To solve it, the shared library loader must be able to deduce the dependency between static objects, which is almost impossible considering that dependencies can arise after multiple levels of indirect function calls—especially virtual functions calls whose targets cannot be known at load time.

Because you can't count on things to work at static constructor time unless they are specifically documented to do so—and most should not make that promise— avoid exporting static objects as part of an interface that can be called from static object constructors (this is also important for performance reasons, as described earlier). For more information, see "Avoid static objects" on page 58.

✔ NOTE   *The Annotated C++ Reference Manual* (Stroustrup) discusses a technique (not based on static objects) that achieves much of the same benefit as static objects but doesn't suffer from this problem. Read §3.4, "Start and Termination," if you are thinking about exporting static objects to clients.

THE C PREPROCESSOR

Though the C preprocessor is one of the most powerful features of C and C++, avoid using it. Except for #include files, preprocessor symbols, and conditional compilation, C++ has features that supersede most of the techniques that required the C preprocessor. Sometimes you need to use the preprocessor to accomplish things you can't with C++, but the need occurs far less often than when using straight C. For example, the Taligent Application Environment uses macros in some places to create meta-information that cannot be found via the current, interim runtime. Be careful though—the Taligent Development System restricts how you can use the preprocessor.

Use const **instead of** #define **constants**

Never use #define for symbolic constants. Instead, use the C++ const storage class. As with #define symbols, const declarations are evaluated at compile time (for types and expressions that qualify as compile-time constants). Unlike #define symbols, they follow the C scope rules and have types associated with them. You can also use enum to prevent a host of problems. For example:

```
#define kGreen 1                // Bad
const int kGreen = 1;           // Better
enum Color {kRed, kGreen, kBlue}  // Best
```

If you accidentally redefine a name with a #define, the compiler silently changes the meaning of your program. With const or enum you get an error message. Even better, with enum you can put the identifiers in the scope of a class (see "Use global names only for classes" on page 35). As an added bonus, each enumeration is treated as a separate type for purposes of type checking (much like the way scalars are handled in Pascal) and for purposes of overloading.

Unlike in ANSI C, objects in C++ that are declared const and initialized with compile-time expressions are themselves compile-time constants (but only if they are of integral or enumeration type). Thus, they can be used as case labels or in compile-time expressions.

**Use enum instead
of sets of constants**

If your constants define a related set, don't use separate const definitions. Instead, make your constants an enumerated type. Remember to document whether the constants may be added to an enumerated type in subsequent releases. Absence of comment implies that the set is unchanging for all eternity.

Bad definition style ——————
```
const int kRed = 0;
const int kBlue = 1;
const int kGreen = 2;
```

Best style ————————
```
enum ColorComponent {kRed, kBlue, kGreen};
```

This causes ColorComponent to become a distinct type that the compiler type-checks. Values of type ColorComponent are automatically converted to int as needed, but integers can't be changed to ColorComponents without a cast. If you need to assign particular numerical values, you can do that too:

```
// kBlue and kGreen do not need explicit values because they are
//  assigned increasing values automatically. However, it doesn't hurt.
enum ColorComponent {kRed = -1, kBlue = 0, kGreen = 1};
```

The type declaration should occur within the scope of a class. Then, references to the constants outside of the class' member functions must be qualified:

```
class TColor {
public:
    enum ColorComponent {kRed, kGreen, kBlue};
...
}

foo = TColor::kRed;
```

✅ NOTE   Until recently the enum type name wasn't local to the class; only the actual constants were; the enum type name wasn't qualified. The ANSI base document now states that such type names (indeed all nested type definitions) are local to the class' scope and must be qualified. Thus, the variable foo in the last example was previously declared as a ColorComponent, but must now be a TColor::ColorComponent.

Another language limitation is that compile-time constants other than enum can't have class scope—they must be global. It is illegal to have an initializer for a static class member in the class declaration. However, it is legal to have a static const data member that has a definition elsewhere—such a member is a compile-time constant, but its definition must appear before its use (such as in a header file); otherwise, it isn't usable as a compile-time constant.

Though you can use enum to achieve the same effect, use global constants rather than abusing enum when something must be a compile-time constant. The new C++ namespace feature might ameliorate this problem when it is available in compilers.

Use inlines instead of function macros

Don't use function macros; they are problematic. Instead, declare the functions inline to obviate the need for function macros (see "Inline functions" on page 62 for restrictions). Like const, inline functions follow the C++ scope rules and allow argument type-checking. Both member functions and nonmember functions can be declared inline. Consider this classic example:

```
#define SQUARE(x) ((x)*(x))

// and...

SQUARE(y++);          // y incremented twice
```

When written as an inline, it is actually more efficient than the macro version. What's more, it's correct.

```
inline int Square(int x)
{
    return x*x;
};

Square(y++);          // y incremented once
```

Use templates for specialized functions and classes

One use for the C++ preprocessor was to generate classes and other definitions from templates in order to implement genericity. This is now superseded by the C++ template type facility, which is available in the Taligent C++ Compiler. For information about template conventions, see "Class templates" on page 115.

✅ NOTE   For a quick overview of templates, see *The C++ Programming Language* (Stroustrup), or *The C++ Primer* (Lippman). Templates are useful whenever you want to define a family of classes or functions that is specialized for a number of different types, rather than one that works with only a single type. They are also extraordinarily useful for generating boilerplate, for example, generating a derived class in a stereotypical way.

THINGS TO AVOID

The following tips help keep your code readable and maintainable.

Don't use goto

The C++ goto statement is a serious impediment to the maintainability and readability of code. When the visible appearance of code and the control flow correspond, it greatly aids comprehension and correctness. Using goto subverts this. With goto, you must read every line or you don't know what is going on.

A goto completely invalidates the high-level structure of the code.

Returning from the middle of a procedure is similarly suspect. Don't use either of these constructs. If you feel a burning need to do this, consult your architect.

Avoid magic numbers

A *magic number* is any literal written inline rather than defined as a symbol, except for certain distinguished values such as 1, 0, 10, and so on. For example:

```
a &= 0xFFF00000;
b = 42;
```

Always define such literals as identifiers so that you can easily change their values without having to search the code. The most insidious example is sizes of arrays that are hard-coded in the program text. If a change is made to the size of the array, it is difficult to find all the places where it's hard-coded.

**Avoid bit flags
(& and |)**

Use the Taligent-defined Boolean type if you want to keep Boolean flags. Unless saving space is important in a data structure or argument, the code required to interpret single-bit flags is larger and slower than the code to interpret the Boolean type.

✅ NOTE   In the future, Taligent might support `bool`, the new C++ built-in type for Booleans. For now, stick with the Taligent-defined type.

If you need to use sets of single-bit flags, don't use the & and | operators to test and set these flags because doing so is error prone. (More than one bug has arisen from & used instead of |). Instead, use C++'s (and C's) bit-field facility. This lets the compiler allocate the storage and generate the code for testing and setting. Also, the compiler can take advantage of special instructions not accessible via | and &.

The bit-wise operators are useful in cases where bits must be laid out carefully in storage to match some existing definition or hardware registers, rather than left up to the vagaries of the compiler. However, such code is usually not portable and should be isolated. For more information on isolating code, see "Nonportable code" on page 113.

**Avoid using arrays
as local variables
or object fields**

Aside from questions of stack size, arrays used as local variables or object fields must have their bounds determined at compile time. Using arrays with fixed bounds often signals that an arbitrary limit exists in your code. If that limit is exceeded, an exception or possible stack corruption results. If you use large arrays with fixed bounds, consider whether your code is general enough. If you are tempted to think, "Who would ever have more than 100 elements in this array?" please remember a similar query: "Who would ever want more than 64K (or 640K!) of memory in a personal computer?" On the other hand, if the size of your array is derived from the log of the number of elements you deal with (because, for example, it is a stack for a recursive algorithm) and it has 100 elements in it, you are probably safe.

For more information on storage management issues, see "Storage management philosophy" on page 57.

CHAPTER 4

TALIGENT ENVIRONMENT PROGRAMMING CONVENTIONS

No application seems finished before it has to ship: there are always changes you'd like to make or features you'd like to add. Rather than delay delivery, you make those changes in updates or revisions. To ensure a high degree of certainty that your code will continue to work as your program changes and interacts with other programs, you must establish guidelines to follow as you write code. The conventions and guidelines in this chapter are the construction rules Taligent follows to ensure that code written today will be robust, portable, and extensible in the coming years.

TALIGENT LIBRARIES

When they exist, use Taligent Application Environment library routines rather than the routines defined in the standard ANSI C libraries. Taligent Application Environment routines might have a more efficient implementation than their C library equivalents, and Taligent maintains control over their definition, semantics, and performance. For example, use memory allocation routines defined in the class TMemHeap rather than `malloc` and `realloc` (better still, use `new` and `delete` rather than `malloc` and `free`).

Standard C libraries are more generic and are not always aware of conditions that Taligent Application Environment routines must know about. For example, the standard C string functions don't support Unicode properly, and `memcpy()` doesn't handle overlapping moves from lower to higher addresses (use TMemorySurrogate instead).

Avoid homegrown utility classes

Taligent doesn't permit its engineers to use homegrown alternative utility classes in code that Taligent supplies. The Taligent Utility classes provide a complete spectrum of support, from the very general collection classes to a set of primitive data structure classes that are very efficient. These latter classes have largely inline implementations where it counts, and are just as efficient as a hand-coded alternative.

Given that reuse of code is one of the driving principles of the Taligent Application Environment, that reimplementation of standard algorithms is a significant source of bugs (data structure bugs can be particularly hard to track down), and that there is no efficiency imperative, there is no reason to write your own utility class when programming for the Taligent Application Environment. Taligent requires an architect's approval before an engineer may construct data structures that duplicate supplied functions.

Use the Name Server

Use the Taligent Toolbox Name Server to name fixed resources; but don't use it for naming user-visible entities. Think of it as naming C++ static variables, rather than instances of objects. Like static variables, the servers named in the Name Server have fixed names that are hard-wired into client code (in their client objects). Object instances, on the other hand, don't necessarily have names, and the way they are identified varies from subsystem to subsystem. If you have multiple instances of servers that act like object instances, or that correspond to an open-ended set of user-visible entities (such as mounted file system volumes or disks), consider using an alternative way of identifying them.

Although it's technically possible for the Name Server to map server identifiers into a character string, don't do it. The Name Server's database needs to be resident, and you have to rework the server startup code to dissociate the server name from the program name—it is hard to uniquely map to and from strings.

✅ NOTE   Eventually a more powerful local Name Server that uses objects as keys and values will replace the current Name Server. The current Name Server API will continue to be supported as an alternative interface.

STORAGE MANAGEMENT PHILOSOPHY

Storage management is a real burden. The best rule of thumb to make life easier is *don't do it*: use automatic or static allocation instead. Failing that, follow the guidelines given in this section for managing your storage.

Hide allocation inside a class

If you have to allocate storage, do so inside a class where it is easy to track. For example, THashTable allocates subsidiary data structures (the hash table) that are invisible to clients. You can also use a surrogate that does reference counting to allocate and deallocate real objects (see "Surrogate objects" on page 91).

Don't assume use of a heap

When writing an interface, don't assume that objects that get passed in are on the heap, because this method doesn't work well for objects on the stack. If you must assume that an argument is heap based, document that fact; and if you plan to take responsibility for managing the storage, use the proper naming convention. Begin the function name with *Adopt...*, as explained in "Name conventions" on page 32.

Clarify ownership of storage in interfaces

Make storage management implications clear to the callers of an interface, especially if the routine allocates storage for which the caller must take responsibility. The names for these routines must begin with *Create...*, *Copy...*, or *Orphan...*; if they take responsibility for arguments, they begin with *Adopt....* Make these issues explicit by using comments, naming conventions, and documentation.

Don't use very large local variables or members

Auto (local) variables and members of objects that are themselves auto variables are allocated on the stack. However, stack sizes are platform dependent, and in a layered environment, the thread stack sizes can be up to the host operating system. Large data structures can blow the stack as your program moves between platforms and hosts.

Conversely, if you decide to place large objects on the heap, you might notice that it takes several hundred microseconds to allocate them. Follow these guidelines when trying to determine whether to put a variable on the stack (as part of another object) or on the heap:

Don't allocate more than a few kilobytes at a time on the stack. This is a rule of thumb, and you'll have to use your best judgment. Think of it as the point where you should start wondering whether something should really be on the stack. Talk to an architect if you have questions. In addition, avoid algorithms that use recursion in an unbounded fashion, as the default stack always has some preset size. Algorithms that use recursion in a bounded fashion, such as Quicksort, are acceptable. The deeper you recurse, the less stack space you should use on each recursion.

Use the heap for larger objects, not the stack, regardless of performance. There are a number of custom storage allocation techniques you can use (such as pooling objects for reuse) to cut down on the overhead for large heap objects.

For information about memory issues with local arrays, see "Avoid using arrays as local variables or object fields" on page 53.

SHARED LIBRARIES

Shared libraries have many advantages, including easy software updates, code sharing, and the ability to dynamically load objects. However, they have one disadvantage: because the library is shared among many applications, unreferenced code and data can't be stripped. This is a minor problem for code, because it is immutable and is shared among all clients. Additionally, unused code doesn't get paged in, and the segmentation capabilities of the Taligent Linker segregate code into contiguous *chunks* that are used together to reduce fragmentation. Static data, however, is a problem.

Avoid static objects

Avoid modifying static data because the page it is on will no longer be shared. This is not an absolute rule; it's all right to have modifiable static data or static objects with constructors in a library, as discussed next.

The best way to avoid modifying static data is to not have it in a shared library. This includes static objects with constructors, because the constructors run after library initialization and modify the storage for the object, resulting in a separate copy for each task (plus anything else on the same page). Static objects or struct's initialized by C-style initializers can be shared between all tasks.

If you need static data that is modifiable or is an object, allocate it on demand. For example, rather than having a static array, have a static pointer, and allocate the array the first time it is needed. The same is true for objects with constructors; allocate them as needed. One useful trick is to place static objects inside functions rather than at file scope; then they are initialized the first time the function is called. This works for heap storage as well:

```
void TFoo::Bar()
{
    static TBaz *gWhatever = new TBaz();
    ...
}
```

The allocation only happens once. Of course, this is useful only inside one function, but that function can be of the GetWhatever() variety and can be a static member. Destructors for static local objects are called at static destructor time, but with a pointer (as in the example) there is no destructor, so the object is not destroyed automatically. Remember too that there are concurrency considerations for all static variables, including those declared inside a function—such as when more than one thread calls TFoo::Bar().

Modifiable statics in a library

You can have modifiable static data or static objects with constructors in a library. Just remember that they take space, and if they aren't used the space is wasted. If the objects are small and few, that's not a problem compared to the added complexity of allocating them on demand. If they're used frequently, allocating them on demand can take more space for the allocation code. Look at your link map to discover how much space your static objects require. Then look at each static object in your library and ask yourself which ones are used infrequently and how big are they?

It's not a good idea to export static objects with constructors from the interface of your library, because you can run into the infamous *order of execution of constructors of static objects* problem described in "Static object constructors" on page 48 (for a full discussion and ideas on how to work around it, see the next section, "Consider alternatives to temporary objects"). If you try to use an exported static object from your own static object constructor, you have a 50-50 chance of hitting the problem. Thus, it's best to use a different technique. Static objects that don't have constructors or destructors do not have this problem.

Consider alternatives to temporary objects

Constructors, like any function, take time to execute. If you use an object as a constant, it's better to create it once and use it repeatedly. One way to do this is to make the object static. By placing it at file scope, it is implicitly static, or if only used by one function, it can be static inside the function. Unless the class in question relies implicitly on other static objects, this latter technique has the advantage of not falling prey to the dreaded *order of static constructors problem* described in "Static object constructors" on page 48. Unfortunately, it has concurrency implications, whereas an object at file scope does not. So, for example:

Potentially expensive ──────
```
Foo(TToken("Hi Mom"));              // Pay for constructor each time, but safe.
```

Consider this instead ──────
```
TToken hiMom("Hi Mom");             // No concurrency issues, but always
void Bar()                          //  constructed even if never used.
{
    Foo(hiMom);
}
```

Or this ──────
```
void Bar()
{
    static TToken hiMom("Hi Mom");  // NOTE: Potential concurrency problems!

    Foo(hiMom);
}
```

BINARY COMPATIBILITY CONSIDERATIONS

One of the most important goals for the Taligent Application Environment is binary compatibility from release to release. Once your code is released, you may not make changes that break compatibility. This section covers some do's and don'ts to help you achieve this.

Adding virtual and nonvirtual functions

Both the current and final Runtime systems allow you to add nonvirtual functions. Also, the final Runtime system will allow the addition of new virtual functions. See "Virtual functions" on page 66 for more information.

Changing a function from inline to noninline

Although you can do this, changing a function from an inline to a noninline won't affect any of the compiled code that calls it. It only affects new callers. See "Inline functions" on page 62 for more information.

Removing private nonvirtual functions not called by inlines	If you refer to a function from an inline, and clients or derived classes call that inline, *you can never remove the function* or change it from virtual to nonvirtual (or vice versa).

You can remove private functions that are not virtual if the implementation no longer references them. This includes references from inline functions.

You can remove virtual privates (or change to nonvirtual) if you did not specify in your documentation that they can be overridden.

You can change a private function from nonvirtual to virtual, but you must recompile all your own code that calls it.

Using classes internal to your implementation	If you have classes whose definition does not appear in any public header file, you can do anything you want. However, you have to recompile and reship any code that does refer to the class definition.

It's acceptable for the class' name to appear in a public header file if it only appears as a forward declaration (for example, class TFoo;).

Use virtual functions if overrides are possible	Member functions can't be changed between virtual and nonvirtual without breaking callers (except for private functions under some conditions). If you think you might ever want to override a function, make it virtual (unless it's private, in which case you can safely change it to virtual later if it's not called from an inline). It is possible to add a second function that is virtual and have the original one call it, but that's less efficient (you always pay for two function calls).

Rearranging, adding, and removing private data members with restrictions	Private data members can be added, removed, and rearranged only if:

They are not referenced from any public or protected inline function that is available to clients or derived classes (part of the Taligent API or SPI).

Doing so doesn't change the offset of a data member that is referenced from any public or protected inline function. It can be hard to determine the impact on portability, as different processors align data differently. It's not clear at this point whether this includes changing the vtable pointer offset. To avoid this latter problem, declare a virtual function before any data members (always place public declarations first).

Doing so doesn't change the size of the class.

If your class is more complex than the very simplest (such as TGRect), take these steps to leave yourself room for future data expansion.

1 Add a private data member with the following declaration at the beginning of your private declaration section:

```
void *fExtension;                 // room for growth
```

2 Make sure that all of your special member functions (constructors, destructor, assignment, copy constructor, and streaming operators) are defined and *not inline*.

3 If you have to add fields in the future, you can make an extension structure and change the declaration to:

```
TFooExtension *fExtension;
```

After that, because TFooExtension's declaration isn't public, you can do whatever you want to it from release to release (see the next section, "Inline functions"). The disadvantage is that it is allocated on the heap. If you have a class for which that is unacceptable, make sure you will *never* need to grow the size of your class—for example, to add more than one pointer's worth of reserved space.

✅ NOTE   Some C++ runtimes allow you to change sizes of objects without such workarounds, but it is not clear when or if Taligent will support such a feature.

INLINE FUNCTIONS

Avoid inline definitions because they get compiled into your caller's code, making them difficult to revise. For clients to compile a class that contains an inline, they must have the source code for that function. Once the source is in circulation, it cannot be changed without breaking binary compatibility. What's more, if an inline refers to internal details of a class, those details can never change. Because of these ramifications, at Taligent an architect must approve every inline function.

There are times, however, when inlines are acceptable. In each of these cases, the function implementation is *defined* by its declaration.

**Inlines that call
something else**

If your inline function just calls something else that is not inline, it's fine, as long as the other function has, by definition, *identical* semantics. For example, Taligent had a class, MCollectible, that defined a virtual function IsEqual that compared two objects for equality. It also had an inline definition for `operator==`, as a notational convenience. Because `operator==` just called the IsEqual function, it was all right for it to be inline and not virtual. This does *not* apply if your function just happens to have a one-line implementation. Another example is constructors or destructors *declared* empty.

A more subtle question concerns `operator==` versus `operator!=`. Should you define `operator!=` as an inline that just says `!(a==b)`? It would be highly questionable to have this be semantically invalid, as that would confuse clients tremendously.

However, making such an inline declaration precludes supplying a more efficient implementation in the future. Because people often make a test based on the expected outcome, it might be possible to supply custom implementations of == and != that were optimized for expected == and expected !=, respectively. Having an inline implementation of != makes this impossible.

Sometimes having this inline implementation doesn't help, and making the inline declaration saves writing an extra routine (and having extra code). There is a gray line, however, somewhere between the simple case of the same function with two names (like IsEqual and ==) and two substantially different functions. Err on the side of caution; talk to an architect if you are not sure.

The greater the extent that the implementation is in the inline function, the less flexibility you have in the future.

Also, if you have a function in an abstract base class, think about whether it should have an empty implementation or be a pure virtual function. If it must be overridden by subclasses, it should be a pure virtual function. If it's acceptable for it not to be overridden, consider whether you really want the empty definition inline. Remember, you might decide to add default behavior to that function some day; if you've made it inline, you no longer have that opportunity.

**Inline function
definitions in .C files**

Taligent previously advocated putting some inline function definitions in .C files, so that only internal functions would get the inline version (normal clients would call it out-of-line). However, avoid this because *it is not a portable construct.*

An equivalent portable alternative is to have a private inline defined in the header file. Internal clients can call the private inline, and you can provide a public (out-of-line) function for normal clients to call that turns around and calls the inline.

✅ NOTE   As with all inlines, of course, if the function is more than a few lines you should not make it inline.

Inlines for extreme efficiency

Sometimes it's acceptable to use inlines if efficiency is extremely important. However, if you do this, *you can never change this routine once your code ships*, and frequently you do not save that much.

Consider that Taligent's complex number implementation makes addition and subtraction functions inline (fairly short); but, multiplication and division are regular functions because they are longer—the overhead for a call is less important and code size is more important. Here, the efficiency consideration together with the low probability of a future change makes an inline a good idea.

System performance can decrease by making something inline; code size might increase due to duplication of code, and that increases the amount of code that must fit in ROM or be paged off disk. One extra trip to the disk costs around 2,000 subroutine calls (the faster the processor, the more it costs). Also, once a function is longer than a couple of lines, the call overhead is a small fraction of the total time. Additionally, the calling conventions of Taligent's final runtime will make the overhead even smaller. You don't save much by making it inline.

If you don't *know* that your implementation must be inline, *do not make it inline*. Build it normally and then measure the performance. Experience has shown again and again that programmers spend lots of time optimizing code that hardly ever gets executed, while totally missing the real bottlenecks.

✅ NOTE   For more information about inlines and efficiency, refer to *The Psychology of Computer Programming* (Weinberg), and to *Programming Pearls* and *Writing Efficient Programs* (Bentley).

The empirical approach is much more reliable. Although better algorithms or smarter data structures generally buy you a lot more performance than random code tweaking, there is a legitimate role for such inlines, and there are many in the Taligent Application Environment. However, when a Taligent engineer wishes to make a function inline, the engineer must have either a compelling argument or objective performance data to sway the architect to approve it.

Don't write inlines in declarations

C++ has two ways of declaring an inline member function. One is to declare the member function normally and then supply an inline function definition later in the same header file. The other is to write the function definition directly in the class declaration. Don't use this latter form—*always declare the function normally and then put an inline definition at the end of the file*. That way, it's much easier to change between inline and regular implementations of a function, and it's no less efficient. The fact that something is inline should not be obvious in the class declaration because clients might start counting on it.

```
class TFoo {
public:
    int TweedleDee() { return 1; };    // Bad!
    int TweedleDum();                  // Good!
};

inline int TFoo::TweedleDum()
{
    return 2;
};
```

One exception to this guideline concerns functions that are *declared* to be empty
(usually in abstract base classes); you can write these directly in the declaration,
as in:

```
class TFoo {
public:
    virtual ~TFoo() {};                // Declared to be empty
};
```

However, don't do this unless you know you will never, ever change it.

**Inlines for exporting
private and protected
members**

Although inline functions have problems, using them is better than directly
exporting data members as public or protected. For example, you can make a
data member available for reading only via an inline, but not if it is public.
Taligent requires an architect's approval for all such constructs in Taligent code.

**Empty special
members**

If you have an abstract base class with no storage and no implementation, it's
acceptable to make the special member functions explicitly empty in the class
declaration, as shown in the last example (~TFoo() declared to be empty). If
there are any data members or if there is significant implementation, don't do
this. When in doubt, talk to an architect.

**Virtual inline
functions where the
type is not known**

This might strike you as a contradiction in terms, but a virtual inline makes
perfect sense. If the compiler knows the type of the object statically, it's called as
an inline. If the type is not known statically, a virtual function call is made. If you
are using an inline for valid reasons, such as when a pointer or reference is used
to access the object, this can be a useful technique. The this pointer is included,
so calls to virtual inline members of the same object always occur virtually. Recall
that writing MyMember(); is equivalent to writing this->MyMember();.

VIRTUAL FUNCTIONS

Virtual functions allow the system to decide which functions to execute at run time. Use them to defer abstract-operation implementation to a derived class (best), or to allow a derived class to augment the implementation of an operation defined in the base (not as good).

Do *not* use virtual functions to trap calls and then take an action based on where the calls came from. Such traps are often used to handle erroneous conditions in the caller. These mechanisms wreak havoc with the data abstractions and ruin one of the major benefits of object-oriented programming. If you override a function, the override must make sense in terms of the definition of the function itself and that of its class.

Virtual functions inherently allow function calls to cascade back through the base classes—for example, DerivedDerived::Foo calls Derived::Foo, which calls Base::Foo. To avoid cascading calls to inherited functions, define an empty *hook* function. If it is called inside the base class only, make the hook function a private virtual. You can make it protected, but that solves the problem only for the first derived class. Subsequent classes must know whether to call the inherited hook.

A function must make sense in terms of the object to which it belongs, without any reference to its possible callers or when they might call it.

Define class abstractions

For the client to be able override a virtual function, you must make a clear definition of what the function does, even if the client only calls the inherited version after a little processing. The class must specify whether and how virtual functions can be overridden, and what the derived class' responsibilities are.

The presence of `virtual` or `protected` is not enough to define the interface seen by a derived class, just as a class definition by itself is not enough to specify the interface seen by clients. The interfaces seen by clients and derived classes have a semantic component as well as a syntactic one; the C++ syntax often expresses only a small fraction of the total interface. If a function can be overridden, you must state so explicitly in the class specification (unless it's a pure virtual function). Your interface must be thought through and well documented. The next two sections go into more detail.

Decide now what might be overridden later

Because the calling site for a function must execute different code depending on whether it is virtual or not, it is not possible to change a function from virtual to nonvirtual, or vice versa, without breaking binary compatibility. Therefore, *any class that might allow polymorphism in the future should use virtual functions now,* and *any function that will eventually allow overriding should be virtual now.* This is true even if derived classes and overriding are not allowed now. Because this is an irrevocable decision, it's better to pay the few extra cycles and reserve the option to allow derived classes later. (Virtual function calls in the Taligent Runtime system have very low overhead relative to regular function calls.)

Remember, making something virtual does not mean it can be overridden; whether and how member functions can be overridden must be stated in the class definition.

Of course, if you are sure that you will never have derived classes, or that a given function should never be overridden, you don't need to make your functions virtual. You can find examples in the Taligent Application Environment, including TGPoint, TToken, and the `complex` class. And if your class can afford an extra function call, you can add a virtual version later and have the nonvirtual version call it.

⬤ NOTE   Inline functions can be virtual. When the compiler knows the type of the object at compile time, it generates the inline; when it does not (such as when a pointer or reference is used), it calls the function through a virtual dispatch. See "Virtual inline functions where the type is not known" on page 65 for more on this.

When to use pure virtual functions

The presence of the keyword `virtual` does not mean that a function can be overridden. This must be explicitly stated in the class specification. A pure virtual function, however, is an exception. Declare a pure virtual function like this:

```
class TAbstract {
public:
    virtual void MustOverride() = 0;
};
```

Before a concrete class (one that can be instantiated) can be created, all pure virtual functions that it contains must be overridden. This is valuable both for documentation and for forcing compile-time checking.

Private virtual functions to control access

C++ has access control, but not visibility control. This means that private functions are visible but not accessible. A private virtual function can be overridden by derived classes, but can only be called from within the base class. This is actually a useful construct when you want that effect.

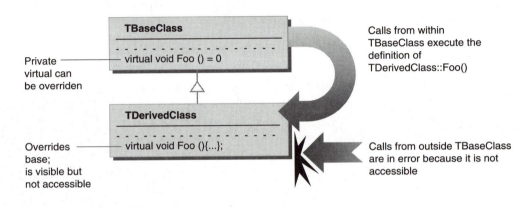

Base class constructors cannot call virtual functions

When a base class constructor is executing, the object is a *base class object*. Any virtual function calls execute the base class virtual functions, not the overriding functions in the (as yet unconstructed) derived class. But sometimes some initialization associated with the base class must be done using derived class (overriding) virtual functions. To handle such a case, it is necessary to call a special virtual function immediately after constructing the instance. Always name this type of function *Initialize*.

✅ NOTE   Derived classes only override Initialize() if they want to add their own post-construction initialization calls.

For example, sometimes during construction you need to create items that can't be created until the most derived class is constructed. Suppose you have a guard element of a linked list, where overridding DoMakeLink() in a derived class can change the type of the link element. By postponing the Initialize() call to the most derived constructor, you call the proper DoMakeLink.

Never require the client to call a separate virtual Initialize() function to finish initialization after constructing all bases. Requiring the client to remember this is extremely error prone; if the client forgets, the object will not be properly constructed.

The cost of failing to call Initialize()

The overhead of checking for failure to call Initialize() is comparable to or greater than the following alternative schemes for achieving the same end:

Lazy evaluation. In every client function, check a flag (set to FALSE in the constructor); then complete initialization by calling the virtual initializer at that time. This works well only in a limited number of cases.

External/internal constructors. Classes in the hierarchy affected by the need for virtual initialization should have both internal (protected) and external (public) constructors. The internal constructors don't call virtual Initialize(). The external constructors call the internal one (actually, a shared private function), as well as the internal constructors of all bases. The external constructors then call the virtual Initialize(). This is error prone too, but only for subclasses as opposed to all clients.

Clients call the external constructor, and derived classes call the internal constructors of their base classes. This method calls the virtual Initialize() for the most derived class only, the one the client constructed directly.

```
class Base {
public:
    Base() {InitBase(); Initialize();};
protected:
    virtual void Initialize();
    enum {kInternal} InternalMarker;
    Base(InternalMarker) {InitBase();};
private:
    void InitBase();
};

class Derived: public Base {
public:
    Derived() : Base(kInternal) {InitDerived(); Initialize(););
protected:
    virtual void Initialize();
    Derived(InternalMarker) {InitDerived();};
private:
    void InitDerived();
};
```

Use virtual base class semantics. Include a virtual base class in the affected class hierarchy, and make use of the fact that only the outermost call to that base class' constructor is used. The Taligent Application Environment will include a class similar to this:

```
#include <typeinfo.h>
#include <stdio.h>
class VInitialize {
public:
    VInitialize(const typeinfo& t) : fCompleteType(t) {}
    void CheckForInitialize() { if (typeid(*this) == fCompleteType) Initialize(); }
    void CheckForFinalize() { if (typeid(*this) == fCompleteType) Finalize(); }
    virtual void Initialize() = 0;
    virtual void Finalize() = 0;
private:
    const typeinfo& fCompleteType;
};
```

Class that does not care about special initialize/finalize

```
class Base {
public:
    Base() {}
};
```

First class that cares

Only called if this is the complete class

```
class JoesParent : public Base, public virtual VInitialize {
public:
    JoesParent() : Base(), VInitialize(typeid(JoesParent)) {
        CheckForInitialize();        // normal initialization
    };
    ~JoesParent() {
        CheckForFinalize();          // normal finalization
    }
protected:
    virtual void Initialize();        // only called if this is the complete class
    virtual void Finalize();          // only called if this is the complete class
};
```

```
class JoeClass: public JoesParent {
public:
    JoeClass() : JoesParent(), VInitialize(typeid(JoeClass)) {
        CheckForInitialize();        // normal initialization
    }
    ~JoeClass() {
        CheckForFinalize();          // normal finalization
    }
protected:
    virtual void Initialize();        // only called if this is the complete class
    virtual void Finalize();          // only called if this is the complete class
};
```

```
void JoesParent::Initialize() { puts("Called JoesParent::Initialize()"); }
void JoesParent::Finalize()   { puts("Called JoesParent::Finalize()"); }
void JoeClass::Initialize()   { puts("Called JoeClass::Initialize()"); }
void JoeClass::Finalize()     { puts("Called JoeClass::Finalize()"); }
```

```
int main() {
    puts("--- creating a JoesParent ---");
    JoesParent *x = new JoesParent;
    puts("--- creating a JoeClass ---");
    JoeClass *y = new JoeClass;
    puts("--- deleting a JoesParent ---");
    delete x;
    puts("--- deleting a JoeClass ---");
    delete y;
    return 0;
}
```

Output

```
--- creating a JoesParent ---
Called JoesParent::Initialize()
--- creating a JoeClass ---
Called JoeClass::Initialize()
--- deleting a JoesParent ---
Called JoesParent::Finalize()
--- deleting a JoeClass ---
Called JoeClass::Finalize()
```

Destructors are not automatically virtual

A class must have a virtual destructor if it has any virtual functions, or if it is deleted through a polymorphic pointer. Destructors are not automatically virtual in classes that have other virtual functions. If you delete such a class through a pointer to one of its bases, the derived class destructors are not called unless the destructor is virtual. So, as with any other member function that you want to call through a base class pointer, the destructor must be virtual if you want the right one to be called.

Remember also that any virtual functions called from a constructor or destructor resolve to the implementation of the class whose constructor or destructor is being executed. This is because any derived class' state has not yet been constructed or has already been destructed. For more information, see "Base class constructors cannot call virtual functions" on page 68.

Switch statements indicate polymorphism

Any time you find yourself writing code that looks like "If it's an A, do this; if it's a B, do that; if it's a C…," reconsider your design. If A, B, and C all have a common base class, that base class needs a virtual function that each subclass can override. You then call that virtual function instead of your switch statement.

Switch statements are nature's way of saying that you should be using polymorphism. The same thing applies to lookup tables.

This applies even when you're trying to create an object. If you have a set of objects, and you want to create an object that corresponds to an object in that set, ask the first object to create the new object. The alternative—testing the object type and creating the second object on that basis—is not extensible when new types of objects are introduced.

Consider video device configuration. Different video devices have different capabilities. For this reason, the user interface for configuring a video device is highly device dependent. Some devices are not frame buffers; to those, concepts like bit depth are meaningless. Rather than query the device to figure out what kind of user interface to use ("Are you a frame buffer? How many bit depths do you have?"), have the video device return a user interface object via a virtual member function. The function can even return an object that can later create that user interface object—a *reference* surrogate. For more information, see "Surrogate objects" on page 91.

This does not imply that every video device must implement its own user interface. If most devices have common characteristics, Taligent might provide a standard user interface object for most devices to return. This way you can handle devices with special requirements without having to revise the system to know about them.

✅ NOTE   Classes used at boot time must be careful about referring to classes that, in turn, refer to things in high-level shared libraries. Using indirect reference objects alleviates that problem.

When to use virtual assignment

Assignment, or `operator=`, is a function that requires careful consideration before you make it virtual. You might think that, like other members, it is better to make it virtual to be safe. Otherwise, you run into problems like this:

```
void Bar(TFoo &arg)
{
    arg = value;
}
```

If `TFoo::operator=` is not virtual, this assignment will slice the object. So shouldn't assignment always be virtual?

There is a catch. Because C++ automatically overloads assignment in each new class, you need to supply two assignment operators. If you have a base TBase and its derived class TDerived, and TBase has virtual `operator=`, then TDerived might need to override `TBase::operator=`, in addition to defining its own `operator=`. If

TDerived defines virtual `operator=`, its subclasses must override
`TBase::operator=` and `TDerived::operator=`, in addition to defining their own
`operator=`. And so on.

Clearly this gets out of hand quickly. It only makes sense to make assignment
virtual when there are additional restrictions that keep this geometric
progression from occurring.

Consider a shallow class hierarchy, where the classes are convertible between
each other. See the discussion of TColor in "Equality" on page 86 for an
example. Another example is TText; different subclasses should be convertible
among themselves, and the class hierarchy is unlikely to get deep.

Another possibility is that the inherited virtual `operator=` would rarely be
overridden. Overriding happens only if the base class implementation is
adequate in most cases (unlikely), or if it is implemented in terms of other virtual
functions that subclasses do override. This latter method is better than
overriding `operator=` itself because the other virtual functions do not
automatically get overloaded by the compiler in every subclass.

There is also an issue with implementing derived class assignment. Usually, when
you do this, you invoke the assignment operator of your base class (or classes).
However, if your base class does have a virtual `operator=`, or if the base's
`operator=` is otherwise defined to work correctly for all derived classes (for
example, it calls virtual functions to do all the work), you must be careful when
writing `operator=` for derived classes. If you call the base class version too, the
assignment will likely occur twice! In this situation, you need to think of the
derived class assignment as a special case where more specific argument types are
known. If special case handling is not necessary, the derived version can just call
the base class version:

```
TDerived& TDerived::operator=(const TDerived &d)
{
    TBase::operator=(d);
}
```

Always supply an assignment operator in such cases, because the default version
C++ supplies will surely do the wrong thing: in addition to calling the base class
operator, it will copy all your data members.

On the other hand, if a class is going to be used in situations where references
are likely to be assigned to, either the base class `operator=` must always work or
assignment has to be virtual. Otherwise, clients get sliced objects, which leads to
subtle bugs.

This is an area of C++ where there is no single *correct* approach. Theoretically, the
right thing is to always make assignment virtual, but doing so leads to problems of
its own. Because of these trade-offs, whether to make assignment virtual is
something you should consider carefully, in consultation with an architect.

FRIEND FUNCTIONS AND CLASSES

The `friend` declaration lets a class specify that a function or class has access to its private or protected members. Avoid `friend` declarations for loosely coupled classes because they control access at a very coarse granularity and don't specify what's acceptable and what's not (unless you document it). Taligent's preferred alternative is to define *internal use only* public member functions and denote with a comment what they are for (see "Class definition conventions" on page 37).

Friends make perfect sense for some situations, such as tightly coupled classes like TSetOf and TSetIteratorOver from the Collection classes. These classes are implemented in tandem and must know about one another's implementation, so it's appropriate to make them friend classes. Also, overloaded operators or functions must sometimes be global for symmetry, and therefore often must be declared as `friend`. A Taligent engineer must confer with an architect before making `friend` declarations.

EXCEPTION HANDLING

The Taligent Application Environment uses exceptions, not error codes, to deal with unusual circumstances. Exceptions are more robust than error codes; your application should not define error codes, and functions should not signal status by returning them. Exceptions are part of C++ and are described in *The C++ Programming Language* (Stroustrup).

✅ NOTE   For a good discussion of the design issues for C++ exception handling, and for reasons why exception handling is superior to error codes, see Chapter 9 of *The C++ Programming Language* (Stroustrup), and pages 149 through 176 of "Exception Handling for C++," in *1990 Usenix C++ Conference Proceedings*.

Exceptions checklist

1. Learn how exceptions work.
2. Recover resources.
3. Design your exceptions.
4. Know when to throw.
5. Know when to catch.

Exceptions syntax

To review, you throw an exception by saying:

```
throw anException;
```

And you catch it like this:

```
try {
    ...code that might throw an exception;
}
catch (const TFooException &a) {
    ...handle a foo exception;
}
catch (const TBarException &a) {
    ...handle bar exception;
}
catch (...) {
    ...handle anything else;
}
```

The type of anException and the argument lists to the catch clauses can be any type; but the Taligent Application Environment convention is to throw an instance of a non-const TStandardException subclass, and to catch it by const reference to avoid slicing. A catch clause is found by searching up the stack until a clause is found that matches the type of the exception (using the C++ function selection rules, based on anException's static type).

Exceptions can be thrown anywhere, including inside catch clauses. A special case that is only valid inside a catch clause (or functions called from a catch clause) is:

```
throw;
```

This rethrows the exception being processed with the same type as originally thrown (useful when you don't know the exact type, and you often won't). Note that saying

```
throw arg;
```

(where arg is the argument to your handler) does not work, because throw uses the static type. If arg is a reference, you'll slice the object.

Avoid interface specification

One syntactical element you should not use is the *interface specification*, see §9.6 of *The C++ Programming Language* (Stroustrup). This specifies, in a function declaration, those exceptions the function can throw. It looks like this:

```
void Foo(int) throw(a, b, c);
```

If an exception that is not in the list is thrown, the default action is to terminate the program. Because exception handling should be robust against errors, this is counterproductive. To correctly use this feature, you must list all unhandled exceptions that can be thrown by any called function (direct or indirect); this is impractical. For example, a disk error might cause a high-level application action to be unsuccessful. If you use interface specification, *disk error* must appear in every function declaration in the call chain.

Any exception thrown by the Taligent Application Environment should be a descendant of TStandardException, so assume that any function can throw a TStandardException (similar to Stroustrup's hypothetical *Fail* exception). After all, you can always do something sensible with a TStandardException, including produce an error message.

Taligent engineers use interface specification only with an architect's approval.

Perform resource recovery

The great majority of exception-handling concerns center on recovering resources when your function is terminated due to an exception. Most handlers just do resource recovery and then pass the exception on.

Automatic objects

The easiest way to handle resource recovery is to tie it to *automatic objects* (stack-allocated, of storage class auto). An automatic object lives within the scope of the function, and its destructor is called if it still exists when the function is terminated. By tying your resource allocation to the lifetime of an automatic object, you do not have to explicitly catch exceptions.

For example, TMonitorEntry, which is used to acquire a monitor lock, can be allocated on the stack within the scope of the lock. If you exit the scope because of an exception, the lock is automatically released:

Scope within which monitor lock will be held ——————

Lock automatically released, including when exception is raised ——————

```
void aFunction() {
//...
     {
         TMonitorEntry anEntry(myMonitor);
         //... do stuff ...
     }
//...
}
```

Automatic cleanup also applies to base classes and members of an object under construction. If the constructor encounters an exception, it calls the destructors for those base classes and members that have already had their constructors called. The body of your constructor never executes if a base class or data member throws an exception from within its constructor.

✅ NOTE   The ISO/ANSI draft specification is currently silent on what happens if an exception occurs during the execution of the constructor in new TFoo;. According to the constructor rule, any base or member objects with completed constructors will have their destructors called. But there is a storage leak, because no pointer is returned (evaluation of the expression is terminated). The prevailing opinion is that operator delete should be called automatically in such situations because there is no other way to completely recover. Taligent expects ISO/ANSI to adopt this specification; the Taligent C++ Compiler is implemented this way.

```
void f() {
    TFoo *t = 0;
    try {
        t = new TFoo;
    } catch (...) {
        // t == 0 still
    }
}
```

The problem is that allocation happened, but the constructor failed

Also consider the TPrimitiveTypeArray template class from the Collection classes. Unlike a variable length C array that you heap-allocate yourself, there's no need to free the array storage if the TPrimitiveTypeArray is on the stack because the destructor cleans it up automatically.

✅ NOTE   Heap storage isn't the only resource that must be released when there is an exception. The rest of this section goes into greater detail, especially the discussion of TJanitor on page 80.

Stroustrup also discusses cleanup using automatic variables in §9.4 of *The C++ Programming Language*. This is the easiest method if you can cast your resource allocation and deallocation in this form. Otherwise, you must explicitly handle exceptions; the remainder of this section discusses a few guidelines.

Passing exceptions

Most handlers just do resource recovery and then pass the exception on. In keeping with that observation, such handlers should look like the following. (For information on when to try to recover from an exception, see "When to recover an exception" on page 83.)

```
catch (...) {
    ... do your cleanup ...
    throw;
}
```

Place your handlers where you allocate resources in your function. One style is to have many little handlers with cleanup code specific to the resources in that allocated scope:

One technique

```
void Foo() {
    TBar *p1, *p2, *p3;

    p1 = new TBar;
    try {
        p2 = new TBar;
        ...
        try {
            p3 = new TBar;
            ...
        }
        catch (...) {
            delete p2;
            throw;
        }
    }
    catch (...) {
        delete p1;
        throw;
    }
    delete p1;
    delete p2;
    delete p3;
}
```

As you can see, the previous example is rather messy. Following is a better organizing technique that takes advantage of the fact that you can delete a nil pointer (see "Use nil pointer deletion" on page 106 for more information):

Better technique

```
void Foo() {
    TBar *p1=NIL, *p2=NIL, *p3=NIL;

    try {
        p1 = new TBar;
        p2 = new TBar;
        p3 = new TBar;
        ...
    }
    catch (...) {
        delete p1;
        delete p2;
        delete p3;
        throw;
    }
    delete p1;
    delete p2;
    delete p3;
}
```

You still have to include the *normal* deletes of p1, p2, and p3. There's no good way to avoid this problem, unless you don't need access to local variables, in which case you can call a common function to handle it.

Even if your cleanup doesn't involve deleting a pointer, you can use a similar technique with your own flag variables to indicate something needs cleaning up. Although the previous example comes out better with such flags, sometimes nested try blocks are more appropriate (though deep nesting is hard to read and understand); one size does not fit all.

TJanitor

This simple example illustrates an even easier way to handle the storage allocation by using objects. If you have a helper class declared like this:

```
template <class A> class TJanitor {
public:
    TJanitor( A* anA ) : p( anA ) {};
    TJanitor() : p( NIL ) {};
    ~TJanitor() { delete p; };
    TJanitor& operator =( A* anA ) { p = anA; };// Should throw exception if not NIL
    operator A*() { return p; };               // convenience
    A* operator ->() { return p; };            // convenience
private:
    A* p;
    TJanitor( const TJanitor& );               // no copies
    TJanitor& operator=( const TJanitor& );    // no assignments
};
```

Then you can use it like this:

```
void Foo() {
    TJanitor<TBar> p1, p2, p3;

    p1 = new TBar;
    p2 = new TBar;
    p3 = new TBar;
    ...
}
```

As it stands, this class does not implement *smart pointers*, and so doesn't deal with more than one TJanitor pointing at the same object. Smart pointers require considerably more work. The Taligent Application Environment has two classes like TJanitor that you can use: TDeleterFor<> and TDeleterForArrayOf<>.

✅ NOTE   Although the C++ books state that operator new returns 0 when allocation fails, the ISO/ANSI committee has decided to change this to throw an exception, and that is what Taligent implements. This is somewhat moot as it is difficult with a heavily heap-oriented architecture to recover from out-of-memory conditions (at least in the default heap; other heaps are not a problem). Taligent is considering a MacApp-like scheme (prohibit all but critical allocations when available space gets low), but you should still expect operator new to throw an exception.

Design exception classes

All exceptions generated by Taligent Application Environment code descend and inherit from TStandardException. This inheritance ensures sensible error message generation and allows exceptions to stream between tasks. Subclasses of TStandardException represent the actual exceptions or error conditions, and they can be further parameterized by instance variables of the specific class.

The C++ exception mechanism uses inheritance for exception classification.

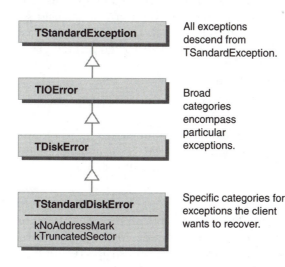

All exceptions descend from TSandardException.

Broad categories encompass particular exceptions.

Specific categories for exceptions the client wants to recover.

> ✅ NOTE   TStandardException is a very low-level class that can safely be used in primitive parts of the system, such as device drivers (assuming the specific subclasses of TStandardException do not have additional dependencies).

What to subclass

As with any interface, make the categorization client driven. The key is to think about what clients want to catch. Categories allow the clients to specify what they think they can recover. As such, introduce a broad base class only when you are sure clients want a uniform way to catch and recover from errors that descend from that base. Don't introduce a base class unless you are sure some clients want to catch and recover from errors that descend from that base in a uniform way.

Similarly, don't specialize a specific exception class unless you think that clients will take different recovery actions based on the distinction you are making. For example, TTruncatedSectorError is probably too detailed because most clients only care that a disk error occurred.

You can always record specific error causes as a data member of your exception subclass. (For example, TDiskError could have an enum member with a getter and setter, and the enum would be over possibilities like kSectorMarkMissing and kTruncatedSector.) In fact, TStandardException contains a handy integer that is intended for that purpose, and the default message formatting code uses it to select the right text. This way the end user is told precisely what the problem is.

| When to subclass | There are two reasons to subclass TStandardException: |

Define a category of exceptions that is handled in a unique way. With your own subclass, clients can catch only the exceptions of interest to them, perform whatever custom cleanup is appropriate, and then rethrow them for standard handling by the Application framework.

Provide scoping for the fetching of error message texts. The error text template is identified by the actual class type (a subclass of TStandardException), and an enum scoped to the subclass. Your subsystem should contain a subclass of TStandardException to which you can add your specific enum value and associated text template.

| Summary | When you are designing your exception classes: |

- Design the class hierarchy to reflect how clients write their catch clauses to recover from errors.
- Group together those errors you recover in the same way. You cannot anticipate all such groupings, but you can reflect the common ones in the hierarchy. Remember that the try-catch syntax allows multiple catch clauses.

When to signal an exception

Signal an exception when a condition occurs that prevents your function from returning its normal result. Of course, part of designing a function is deciding what's a normal result and what's an exception. Stroustrup's rule of thumb is a good one: use exceptions for *exceptional* or *unusual* conditions, not as novel flow of control techniques. Think of an exception as something that has message text explaining the problem associated with it.

✅ NOTE   The Taligent standard requires that all error conditions in the Taligent Application Environment be reported through exceptions, not through error codes.

Destructors

Do not throw exceptions in destructors, and do not call anything that might throw an exception unless you're prepared to catch it and deal with it (see the next section, "When to recover an exception"). Destructors that exit with an exception never finish executing, and the uncleaned resources are lost.

Additionally, the ISO/ANSI draft standard states that if the exit occurs during a stack unwind (while handling an exception), and while searching for an exception handler, the special function terminate() is called. As you might gather from the name, terminate() takes rather draconian measures. Although you can install your own terminate function instead, it cannot be done in a clean way by library software, but must instead be left to the application developer.

When to recover an exception

There are several reasons for recovering an exception:

Try to recover from an exception only when you can take a sensible action. Limit your handlers to fairly narrow categories of errors, with an obvious recovery action. If you do not know what really happened, it is better to let the error surface than to try a random recovery action and hope that the problem goes away. If the recovery action does not work, you might make it worse.

Do not catch TStandardException or (...) and fail to rethrow it. An exception to this rule is in the Application framework, which catches unhandled exceptions, puts up an alert for the end user, and then attempts to continue. Another exception is within the body of destructors. If a destructor does something that can generate an exception, surround that action with a try-catch block that fields any exception (using `catch(...)`) and then attempts to continue. As discussed in the previous section, do not allow an exception to escape from a destructor.

Separate error recovery and resource cleanup handlers occurring in the same function. It is better to avoid resource cleanup inside the error recovery handler because doing so might result in your duplicating cleanup code throughout your handlers. You can nest the recovery handlers inside the try block for the resource cleanup handlers. Or even better, use the technique described in "Automatic objects" on page 76 to avoid resource cleanup handlers altogether. But don't do both in the same handler.

Use assertions to signal error conditions due to programming error, which clients wouldn't want to recover from. A violated assertion drops into a debugger during testing, but throws a standard programming error exception in production use. If the error can occur other than from programmer error, or if clients might want to catch and recover from it, use an exception you define yourself.

PORTABLE HASH

The Taligent Application Environment sometimes stores objects in disk files that are accessed via a hash. Examples of classes that do this are TDiskSetOf and TDiskDictionaryOf. In order for the index structures in these files to work when the files are transported across platforms, the hash functions used must return the same result on every platform.

To do a portable hash, follow these rules:

Only use other portable-hash results or portably converted primitives as elements in your calculations.

Store the hash result as a value; never interpret it as a sequence of bytes.

All of the primitives that you use must be converted to a portable form, with precisely the same results on all machines. This means that you convert all primitive values to HashResult (unsigned long), using only 32 bits.

- For all integer values, this is a simple mask and cast (assume kMask32 is a named constant that stands for the masking value 0xFFFFFFFFU):

```
result = (HashResult) (x & kMask32);
```

This works because:

a. If one operand is unsigned long, the other is converted to unsigned long.

b. If a shorter unsigned value is converted to a longer one, the value is preserved.

c. If a signed value is converted to unsigned, it must have the correct value mod 2^n, where n is the number of bits in the unsigned type. So, a conversion to unsigned long yields identical values on different machines as long as the number of bits in an unsigned long is the same.

d. If the number of bits in an unsigned long is greater than or equal to 32, the least 32 bits of the result in from the previous step (c.) is the same across all such machines.

- For double and float, the Hash supplied by Numerics.h is portable.

```
result = Hash(x);
```

All arithmetic operations that you perform in combining elements must be portable; they must have precisely the same results on all hardware. This means that every operation on HashResult must be masked to 32 bits afterwards. Restrict yourself to the arithmetic operations (+, −, *, /, %) and logical operations (^, &, |, ~, >>, <<, RotateUp, RotateDown).

```
result = (x + y) & kMask32
```

You must guarantee to all clients that you will never change the hashing algorithm, even if there are bugs in it. The only exception to this would be if you had a bug in your algorithm so severe that its prior results were useless. For example, if Hash() returns TRandomNumberGenerator::First(), the old data isn't retrievable. So changing Hash() to return 0 is permissible because it allows new applications to work, while the old ones already don't work.

Strive for uniform distribution

If you want your hash function to return hash values that are uniformly distributed across what the return type can represent, send your result as a seed to a random number generator that returns values of that type. Because the semantics of the random number generator are to return numbers that are uniformly distributed, this makes your hash function also generate values with the same property.

In the future, the Taligent Application Environment will define APIs to assist in computing portable hashes. In the meantime, you might want to write your own helpers, such as a masking function.

Do not implement Hash via member functions

For many objects, Hash (and comparison) aren't intrinsic properties of the objects, but of the collections they are inserted into. Thus, they shouldn't be implemented via member functions. To illustrate why this is a problem, consider TFontIdentifierStyle, which identifies the font to use for text in style sets and line layout. A hash function was added for line layout so that TFontIdentifierStyles could be found. This Hash function was based on the name of the font. However, no one realized that TStyle already defined a Hash function based on the type of the style—it was a TFontIdentifierStyle. So, when this new Hash function was introduced, TFontIdentifierStyles stopped working in style sets.

EQUALITY

Equality between two objects means that the logical contents of the objects are identical in every respect; that is, the two objects can be freely substituted for each other in any context that deals with their values—that excludes address references—without changing the results. As far as the public interfaces are concerned, the two objects always return the same values. The objects can have different internal states that aren't captured in an equality comparison (such as caches or seeds values), but those aren't relevant to the public values of the objects.

- If X==Y, then Y==X.
- If X==Y, and you perform X=Y, then X's behavior should not change in any value context.

Implications

If your comparison compares only one aspect of two objects, name the method accordingly—do not make it an equality operator. (TComparators aren't subject to this restriction, because they explicitly compare only some aspect of the objects.) For example, if your equality operator only ensures that two objects have the same area, you should name it HasSameArea(), *not* ==. If it only ensures that two objects have the same name, it should be HasSameName().

Ensure that your Hash method is coordinated with your equality. The invariant is: if X==Y, then Hash(X) = Hash(Y). For information on Hash methods, see "Portable hash" on page 84.

Watch for subclasses—in the majority of cases two objects of different classes are not equal. Because of polymorphism, you must check the types of classes to get this right. Because runtime type information (RTTI) isn't currently supported, you will generally do this with an MCollectible check (see the "Equality sample" in the next section).

The equality semantics of surrogate classes should depend on whether they act like pointers or act like values. If they act like pointers, they should compare equal if they refer to the same object. If they act like values, they should compare equal if the objects they refer to compare equal.

When equality does not apply

For some classes, equality doesn't make sense and you shouldn't include an equality operator. Perhaps the clearest example is in Taligent's Properties, where there are classes that are named envelopes for other classes that are represented as void*'s. In this case, the envelope can't determine equality among its fields and cannot meaningfully determine when it is equal to another. Other Taligent examples are TView, TStream, TMonitor, and TThreadProgram.

✅ NOTE   Taligent's MCollectible might force you to supply equality; make it very clear with comments and documentation that this is temporary.

One good test is that where assignment doesn't make sense, equality doesn't either. If you cannot define operator=, you shouldn't define operator==.

Equality sample

If different subclasses are always unequal, your equality operator should follow this general form. You can skip step 2 in the following code if your superclass already checks it. If you do have cases where objects of different classes should compare equal, then you have a bit more work to do:

```
// TB inherits from TA
Boolean TB::operator == (const TB& other) const {
    Boolean result;
    // Step 1. fast address check, useful if it occurs often
    if (this == &other) result = TRUE;

    // Step 2. must be same class
    else if (typeid(*this) != typeid(other)) result = FALSE;

    // Step 3. check superclasses ==
    else if (TA::operator!=(other)) result = FALSE;

    // Step 4. fields
    else if (fField1 == other.fField1 && fFieldN == other.fFieldN) result = TRUE;

    return result;
};
```

It is usually more efficient to define operator== as a global function. Do this for the highest class in your hierarchy, where that class' definition should include steps 1 and 2 of the example, and a call to a protected member function PrivateEquality(const TMyClass&). Any subclass then needs to override PrivateEquality to do steps 3 and 4. This makes sure that if X== Y, then Y==X, and avoids making multiple checks in steps 1 and 2.

Equality between different types

If you allow different types to be equal, be very careful that the invariant still holds: if X== Y, then Y==X. Color spaces are an excellent example of equality between different types. The following description explains how assignment works between color space objects of different classes: apply the same sort of conversion lessons to equality.

The Taligent Application Environment supports many color spaces: RGB, XYZ, Gray, and so on. In addition, developers can add new color spaces. Colors can be assigned to each other, even if they are different subclasses of TColor, the abstract base class of all colors. They can also be constructed from each other, effectively converting color spaces. Using colors like value-based objects makes them very developer friendly. For example:

```
TRGBColor rgb( .5, .5, .1);
TRGBColor rgb2( rgb );        // Plain copy construction
rgb2 = rgb;                   // Plain assignment
TXYZColor xyz( rgb );         // Converting construction
xyz = rgb;                    // Converting assignment
```

✅ NOTE   Clients need to note that color conversion can lose precision and is therefore, in general, not reversible; for example, converting an RGB to a GrayColor and back results in a gray RGB color.

Implementation

The trick is to define pure virtual casting operators in TColor which convert any given subclass to a TXYZColor. Any color subclass, therefore, has to know how to convert itself to the canonical XYZ color space.

Also, any color subclass should have a constructor that takes a single TXYZColor argument (unfortunately, this cannot be enforced with pure virtuals). Therefore, subclasses have to know how to do the conversion the other way around (from XYZ to their own type). Once these two things are in place, you can define a pure virtual assignment operator in TColor:

```
virtual TColor& operator=( const TColor& other ) = 0;
```

Its implementation in a typical subclass might look like this:

```
TColor& THLSColor::operator=( const TColor& other )
{
    if( typeid(other) == typeid(*this) )     // Fake RTTI calls
        *this = (const THLSColor&)other;     // Use our assignment
    else
        *this = THLSColor( other );          // Convert and use our assignment
}
```

With real RTTI, `typeid(*this)` can be replaced by `typeid(THLSColor)`.

The optional type check improves efficiency by using a straight (nonconverting) assignment if the two objects are of the same TColor subclass. The else clause deals with polymorphic assignment: the argument is converted to a TXYZColor by the arguments override of the XYZ casting operator. That XYZ color is then passed to the XYZ color constructor of THLSColor. This way, the other color is first up-converted to XYZ (the canonical color space) and subsequently down-converted into the target color space. These conversions aren't necessarily cheap (they can involve matrix multiplies, and so on).

Color subclasses must also have a monomorphic assignment operator (see "When to use virtual assignment" on page 72).

```
THLSColor& THLSColor::operator=( const THLSColor& );
```

You should call this one from the polymorphic assignment implementation, as in the previous example. This avoids having the same thing implemented in two places.

```
// Temporary until RTTI support
#define typeid(x) *((x).GetMetaInformation()->GetClassNameAsToken())

// TColor base class
class TColor : {
...
    virtual TColor& operator=( const TColor& other ) =0;
    virtual operator TXYZColor() const = 0;
...
}

// an example color subclass
class THLSColor : public TColor {
...
    THLSColor( const TXYZColor& other );            // converting ct
    THLSColor( const THLSColor& );                  // monomorphic copy constructor
    virtual TColor& operator=( const TColor& other );  // polymorphic assignment
    virtual operator TXYZColor() const;             // conversion operator
...
    THLSColor& operator=( const THLSColor& other );  // monomorphic assignment
...
}
```

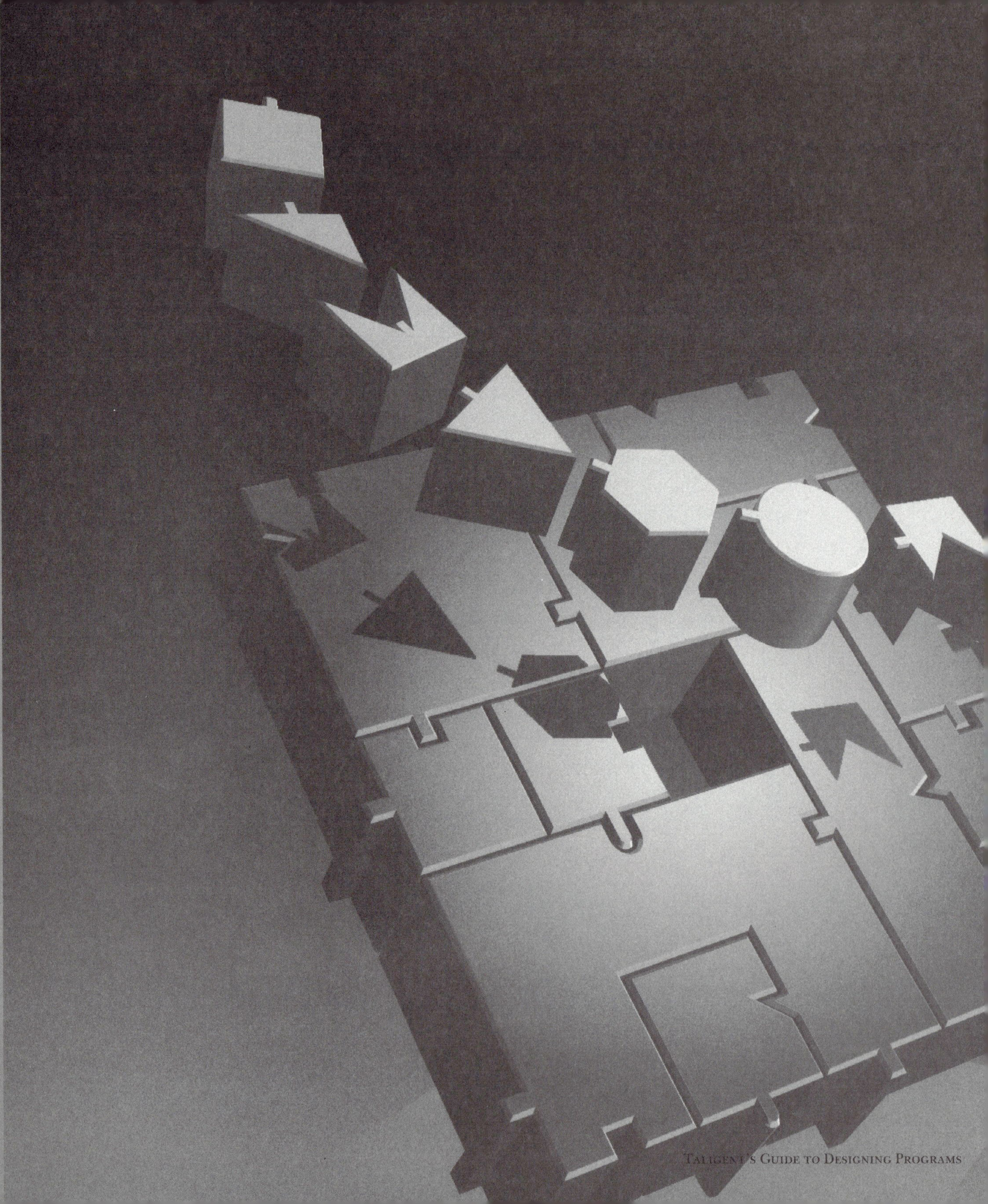

CHAPTER 5

TALIGENT ENVIRONMENT PROGRAMMING TIPS AND TECHNIQUES

No matter how cutting edge your application is, you always draw on the programming skills you learned in previous experiences. This chapter presents tips and techniques to help you avoid some of the common mistakes and subtle gotchas you can encounter while programming for the Taligent Application Environment. You can be sure that at one time or another, each of these topics was the unfortunate misstep, or eye-opening experience, of some fellow programmer.

SURROGATE OBJECTS

Sometimes it is more useful to deal with a reference to an object than to directly create and manipulate the object itself. Other times, it's your only choice, such as for objects in another address space. Objects that act as stand-ins for other objects are *surrogates*. Surrogates are useful in many different situations and can operate in several different ways.

Taxonomy of surrogates   Though it is an incomplete list, this chapter describes five kinds of surrogates:

An explicit master—Where the programmer can create and manipulate a master object, and can also create a surrogate object that can be used to manipulate or refer to the master. Usually, the only way to release resources is to destroy the master. The name for this type of surrogate should be the master object's name, followed by *Surrogate*, as in TFooSurrogate.

A handle to an explicit master—Where the programmer can't explicitly create or manipulate the master object (although this is not a requirement for this model). Instead, creating the surrogate creates a new master object. The semantics are *explicitly shared* semantics, and the master object might be reference-counted and deleted when the last surrogate is destroyed. Because this type of surrogate is a conduit to the real object, end the name of these surrogates with *Handle*, as in TFooHandle. Do this even if TFoo doesn't appear in a public header file.

A hidden master—Where the master object's existence is transparent to the programmer. This is similar to the previous case, but the semantics are *not* shared semantics. Sharing occurs behind the scenes to avoid overhead, but modifying the surrogate object does not modify the master object; instead, a new copy of the master is made and modified (*copy on write* semantics). This surrogate has no specific naming convention because the existence of a master object is transparent to the client. Thus, it's an implementation technique and not part of the class interface. If you have a modifier, put it on the internal class. For example, if the surrogate is TFoo, the internal class is TFooImplementation or TFooStorage or whatever.

A surrogate that views the master—Like the first case, but the surrogate isn't a direct stand-in for the master object. Instead, it is a *synthetic* or *virtual* perspective on that object, a satellite of the master object. It's used to encapsulate information about an aspect of the master object. After a massive thesaurus overdose, the conclusion is that the name for this kind of surrogate depends on the situation. The name of the viewed class should have something in common with the surrogate (for example, TUpdateRegion and TUpdateRequest).

Objects used to get other objects—An object that can be used as a compact reference to another object, which could itself be a surrogate. This surrogate has no protocol other than to obtain the referenced object (which could even be created). The name of this surrogate should end with *Reference*.

Explicit masters

An explicit master surrogate is a stand-in for a master object. While you can access the master object directly, you will probably use the surrogate instead. For example, in the Taligent Application Environment, using the Window Server you can create a TSystemWindow and have surrogate objects that refer to that system window. Only destroying the master object causes the actual resource to disappear. The surrogate nature of the object is visible, and dangling references are possible.

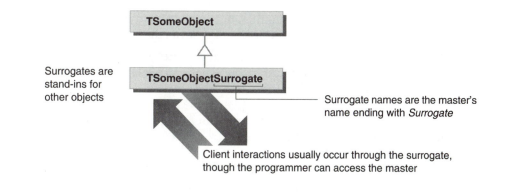

Surrogates are stand-ins for other objects

Surrogate names are the master's name ending with *Surrogate*

Client interactions usually occur through the surrogate, though the programmer can access the master

Handle surrogates

A *handle surrogate* is a conduit you use to get to the master object to avoid direct creation or use of the master object. Use handle surrogates to avoid copying large objects that are too big to pass by value, and where internal use of pointers (rather than copying) is preferable. Some handle surrogates are little more than *counted pointers* wrapped in a class that delegates calls to the master object. Use this technique anywhere that counted pointers are useful—that is, where storage management is difficult due to a multiplicity of references to shared objects.

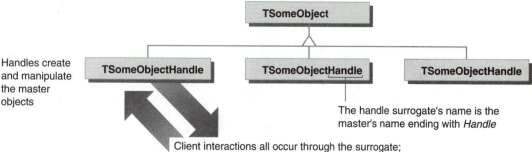

Handles create and manipulate the master objects

The handle surrogate's name is the master's name ending with *Handle*

Client interactions all occur through the surrogate; the programmer can access the master

A handle surrogate is similar to a counted pointer, but because the surrogate has object semantics rather than pointer semantics, it is possible to avoid some of the problems of counted pointers. For example, you can prevent the client from getting hold of a regular C pointer and thus having a dangling reference (which can be avoided with counted pointers, but is a fair bit of work). See "Synchronization techniques" on page 99 for more examples.

Because you don't directly create the master object, the surrogate creates the master when you create the surrogate. Once the master object exists, you can create additional handle objects of the same class that reference that same master. If you are reference counting, the master object exists until the destruction of the last handle, which then destroys the master.

The Taligent Application Environment's kernel interface has such classes as TTaskHandle and TThreadHandle. These have no actual master object (just a reference), and they do not perform reference counting. You must explicitly release the resources they refer to, which can leave dangling references. All such handles need to be safe to use if they contain a dangling reference (for example, throw an exception rather than crash).

Hidden masters

Unlike other surrogates, a *hidden master surrogate* doesn't modify the master object. Instead, it creates and modifies a new copy of the master (*copy on write* semantics); the master's existence is transparent to the client. A Taligent example of a hidden master surrogate is TGArea, which has the hidden master TAreaGeometryHandle.

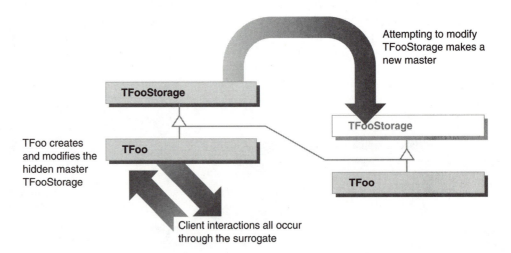

Attempting to modify TFooStorage makes a new master

TFoo creates and modifies the hidden master TFooStorage

Client interactions all occur through the surrogate

A hidden master surrogate's semantics are not shared, although sharing is used behind the scenes to avoid overhead.

Use hidden masters to *lazy evaluate* expensive operations. Clients often copy an area and then modify the copy (rather than the original). However, area-modifying operations frequently need to make a copy of that copy while performing their operations. By using surrogates, you can avoid copying the copy. Instead, the modifying operation creates and modifies another surrogate. It then processes the master objects of both surrogates, and installs the operation result as the master object of the target surrogate.

✓ NOTE   This technique results in a significant reduction of work and you should use it where expensive operations can be delayed or eliminated. Several of the books in the Bibliography discuss this technique.

Be careful using this kind of surrogate in a multithread situation. A caller might make a copy of a surrogate for another thread (not knowing there is a hidden master), and expect that thread to alter its (supposedly) private copy without synchronizing. Because the original surrogate and the copy both point at the same data, there is a potential for a race condition. This problem can be avoided by following these two rules:

Use MReferenceCounted to keep the reference count; it's multithread safe.

Once you create a master object, it must be immutable (you never change it once it is created). There is one exception: for operations that modify the object, you can modify the master directly when the reference count is one. This is because only one caller has the surrogate, and the reference count cannot change during the call because the sole surrogate is busy with the modifying call. This is not true, however, if another thread has an alias to the surrogate (pointer or reference); but this would be an unsafe situation anyway because if a second thread tries to read a surrogate while the first thread modifies it, you have a race condition. Do not share the surrogate; this technique is safe only when you give each thread its own surrogate.

| **Surrogates that view masters** | This kind of surrogate object encapsulates information about an aspect of the master object, but is not necessarily a true surrogate for the master. Instead, it is a synthetic or virtual perspective on that object, and it does not necessarily share a common base class. In the Taligent Application Environment, iterators associated with the Collection classes are such surrogates. |

✓ NOTE   *The C++ Answer Book* (Hansen) also shows an instance of this technique: a SubString class which is a view onto a String class.

Another example of this surrogate is making a bit-vector class that looks like an array of Booleans; specifically, you can use this surrogate to implement the subscript operator. It's fairly easy to define an operator that returns a Boolean:

```
Boolean operator [](int foo);
```

But this can't appear on the left side of an assignment because you can't return a Boolean&—there is no Boolean to return a reference to (remember, it is a bit vector). Instead, define a TBit class that the subscript operator returns:

```
TBit operator [](int foo);
```

TBit has assignment defined for Boolean arguments—TBit& operator= (Boolean)—and also has a coercion operator for changing it into a Boolean— operator Boolean(). It's implemented as a friend class of TBitVector or uses public SetBit and TestBit functions. On assignment of a Boolean, it does a SetBit on the corresponding bit, and it does a TestBit on coercion to Boolean.

The Taligent class TArrayOf uses this technique to return a TArrayOfElement Reference from operator[].

This solution illustrates a powerful technique that the Taligent C++ Compiler does well; but be aware that some compilers generate abysmal code for this.

STORAGE MANAGEMENT ISSUES

In any system that allocates storage dynamically, storage management is an important design issue. This is also true in the presence of garbage collection. However, without garbage collection (as in the Taligent Application Environment), the problem is that much harder. Even though storage management is a design issue, here are some implementation techniques to consider.

Follow naming conventions

If a routine allocates storage that it then hands back to the caller, or if the caller passes storage that the caller is then responsible for, name the function appropriately. See "Name conventions" on page 32 for more information.

Use copy semantics wherever possible

By using the surrogate techniques discussed in "Surrogate objects" on page 91, it's possible to use copy semantics with a reference-based implementation. Of course, this has higher overhead, sometimes too high to allow copy semantics. Even then, it's possible to use reference counting, but be careful to get the implementation right or you will have storage leaks. Use the Taligent MReferenceCounted class to implement reference counting; it is fast and multithread safe.

Although it is possible to reference-count objects without a surrogate object, it's more error prone. The trick is to correctly increment or decrement the count whenever and wherever necessary. Using a surrogate object lets C++ do the work.

A counted pointer can either be exposed directly to clients or embedded inside a surrogate as an implementation technique. Here is a simple example of a counted pointer template to illustrate the technique:

```
template<class T> class TCountedPointer {
public:
    TCountedPointer() { fPointer = NIL;};
    operator T* () const { return fPointer;};              // Dangerous!
    T* operator ->() const { return fPointer;};            // Safer
    TCountedPointer(const TCountedPointer& other)
        { fPointer=other.fPointer; fPointer->AddReference();};
    TCountedPointer(T* p) { fPointer = p; p->AddReference();};
    TCountedPointer &operator =(const TCountedPointer& other)
        {
        T* old = fPointer;
        fPointer=other.fPointer;
        fPointer->AddReference();
        old->RemoveReference();
        };
    TCountedPointer &operator =(T* p)
        {
        T* old = fPointer;
        fPointer=p;
        p->AddReference();
        old->RemoveReference();
        };
private:
    T* fPointer;
};
```

Notice that defining the coercion operator to T* is dangerous because it creates ordinary pointers. Because those ordinary pointers aren't counted, they can become dangling references later on. It is safer to define the appropriate operators on your counted pointer type (unary *, unary ->, and []). Then it's impossible to create an ordinary pointer from a counted pointer. If you additionally override unary & on the actual object to return a counted pointer instead of a regular pointer, you should only have counted pointers. Though it is impossible to prevent references from being used, they are less error prone.

Several references in the Bibliography describe this technique and give more examples.

Avoid storage manipulation in open code

Probably the most error-prone thing you can do in C or C++ is raw storage manipulation. Any time you do pointer arithmetic, calculate lengths of storage blocks, or move them around, you risk an error that is extraordinarily difficult to track down and is among the worst kind of bug to find. Raw storage manipulation (such as storage copying and `sizeof` calculations) should *never* appear in open code; Taligent engineers must talk to an architect first. If you feel that you must do it, here are some guidelines to follow:

Don't do it! Don't try to save time by shortcutting the compiler because you know what it will do and you know a faster trick. When the compiler changes, the assumptions change, or if you get it wrong, you're going to be in hot water.

Use a collection class. The Taligent Collection classes already handle many kinds of storage manipulation including variable length arrays. The primitive forms of the Collection classes are extremely efficient. As an added bonus, the code is shared.

Wrap it in a class. Determine the basic abstraction that requires storage manipulation, and wrap it. That way, you only have to write the storage manipulation code once instead of spreading it throughout your code.

Allocate subobjects on the heap for debugging

As discussed in "Allocate storage only if you must" on page 47, there is no storage allocation overhead if an object can be local to a function. Many objects have very localized scope and do not need to be allocated on the heap.

▶ TIP   When you do early development, it is sometimes useful to allocate subobjects on the heap to avoid some recompilation when their declarations change. Because the subobject isn't inline, the layout of the owner doesn't change when the subobject does. If you do this, make sure you take it out before you release your code.

CONCURRENCY AND SHARED LIBRARY ISSUES

There's an old proverb: "Be careful what you ask for—you might get it." This definitely applies to preemptive multitasking. It solves many problems, but like any panacea, it introduces new ones. The big problem for preemptive scheduling is concurrency and synchronization. If multiple threads are changing or reading data structures at the same time, the chance that the data structures will be consistent is about nil.

One approach is to require that every object in the system be safe for use by multiple concurrent threads. This works, but has a big performance impact and very little benefit. For example, consider an object A, which is built out of other objects B, C, D, and E, which are all safe for use by multiple threads. This does *not* mean that A is therefore safe for use by multiple threads. Although B, C, D, and E all separately preserve their individual invariants, that doesn't mean that A's invariants are preserved. In fact, in making A multithread safe, it is often the case that the components' being multithread safe is of little or no use, as it is A in its entirety which must be synchronized.

Therefore, synchronize high-level constructs only; avoid synchronization at a low level because it has storage and time penalties. There are some exceptions; Taligent's MReferenceCounted is multithread safe because it enables programming that is also multithread safe without any additional overhead (see "Surrogate objects" on page 91). However, the Collection classes are *not* multithread safe because you usually use them to construct other objects, rather than access them directly from multiple threads.

Synchronization techniques

The classic synchronization technique is to use some form of lock. There are two kinds of synchronization locks in the Taligent Application Environment:

- Monitors for synchronizing most data structures with multiple writers. Use monitors except when the semaphore model fits better.
- Semaphores for when there are many readers and one writer. There is less contention, because semaphores directly support multiple readers.

Another technique is to use surrogates (see "Surrogate objects" on page 91). If you can split an object into immutable shared data and per-thread mutable data, you can avoid some of the need for synchronization. For example, TGArea's are not shared between threads, but the master objects they point to are. Only the reference counts in the master objects need to be synchronized, because otherwise they do not change.

✅ NOTE   Synchronization should almost always be performed inside an object, not by clients. Counting on clients to make acquire and release calls is asking for trouble, as they are sure to forget one or the other at some point.

Synchronization and problems with memory access

One assumption people frequently make is that memory accesses are atomic and are therefore safe to use for synchronization. This is definitely *not* true. For example, if you have an `int` variable (declared volatile so that the compiler doesn't put it in a register), you might assume that if the only values written to it are in some set, another thread reading that variable sees one of the values in that same set. That isn't the case, because vagaries in instruction processing and memory subsystems make it possible for the variable to momentarily assume values outside the set when read in an unsynchronized way. Also, writes and reads from different processors on a multiprocessor can appear out of sequence.

In general, it isn't possible to write portable C++ code where multiple threads simultaneously read and write a memory location. Of course, multiple threads can safely read a storage location without synchronization as long as none are trying to write it at the same time. Taligent engineers must consult with an architect before doing so.

Synchronization of global and static variables

Because global and static variables are shared by all threads in an address space, the synchronization considerations apply to them as well. Any globals (including static class members) that are written or read by more than one thread must be protected by locking or other means. An exception is a `const` global with file scope; these are initialized at static constructor time, when only one thread is running, and don't change afterwards.

A particularly insidious problem occurs with static variables defined *inside* functions. Local static variables with an initializer are initialized the first time the function is called, *not* at static constructor time. If more than one thread can make the initial call, they might try to do so simultaneously, resulting in a crash. Local statics are a good way to cut down on overhead, but you must consider this concurrency issue if the function can be called from multiple threads. See "Avoid static objects" on page 58 for more information.

An initializer can be an object's constructor or a primitive type's initializer.

Complex data structures that do not need locking

The idea of accessing data structures without locks is actually an active topic of research these days, and is sometimes called *lock-free synchronization*. Given one or more primitive atomic operations, it is possible to build more complex data structures that do not need locking.

Such primitives include the 68030 Compare-and-Swap instruction and the PowerPC Load-Reserve/Store-Conditional instructions. The Taligent Application Environment runtime uses such techniques to implement the heap allocator. MReferenceCounted also uses this technique on some platforms.

In the future, Taligent might decide to support one or more of these primitives across all Taligent Application Environment systems; then you can write portable code that uses them (the storage allocator has nonportable portions anyway). For now, do not use these constructs without your architect's approval.

If a function can be called by multiple threads, you can only use primitive C types that don't have constructors, such as pointers or numbers, and they must be initialized by compile-time constant expressions; they are initialized before your code starts running. To use an object, you can write code similar to:

```
void Foo() {
    static TBar *gBar = NIL;
    gProtect.Acquire();        // Semaphore can't be function static
    if ( gBar == NIL )
        gBar = new TBar();
    gProtect.Release();
    Function( gBar );          // Safe: above guarantees that gBar is valid
}
```

The semaphore itself can't be static inside the function because it would have the same synchronization problem. If your class is used by multiple threads, you might already have a semaphore or monitor to protect the initialization.

CAUTION   You might be tempted to optimize the previous example by testing for gBar being NIL before you acquire the lock, because the most frequent case is that it has already been initialized. *This is not safe!* Although gBar might be non-NIL, that does *not* mean it has settled into a correct state. Enclosing the initialization sequence in an `if (gBar == NIL)` test makes the function call's reference to gBar unsafe. Unsynchronized access is subtle and dangerous!

Shared memory between tasks

Whenever possible, avoid sharing memory between tasks. Shared memory is often overused, and subsystems using shared memory might not work on secure versions of the Taligent Application Environment or on loosely coupled multiprocessors.

If you have to share memory between tasks, avoid client-writable memory because this greatly compromises the system's reliability. Instead, modify your shared memory from a server, and give clients read-only access. At Taligent, an architect approves all client-writable shared memory.

Shared heaps

Shared heaps in the Taligent Runtime system provide a convenient method for sharing memory. If an object allocates storage and you want the object in a shared heap, use this form of the `new` operator:

```
new(kSameHeap, this) TFoo(arg)
```

This form of `new` is defined as `new(EHeapType, void *, size_t)`, and it allocates the storage in the `void*` argument's heap. If the argument doesn't point to a heap, the allocation occurs in the default heap. This guarantees that any storage this object refers to is going to be in the same shared heap so that it is accessible from all address spaces. Storage allocated in the default heap is accessible only from the address space in which it was allocated.

As with any shared memory, access to objects in your shared heap must be synchronized, unless they do not change once created. For example, if objects built using MReferenceCounted don't change, you need to synchronize the code that locates them, but not the code that uses them. Do any such synchronization with global rather than local semaphores.

Shared memory problems with `const`

The interpretation of `const` in C++ is a matter of confusion. The language defines `const` to mean that the representation of an object does not change. Many people argue that this violates the data abstraction principle that is so important to object-oriented programming—clients shouldn't care if the representation changes, only if the semantic state of the object changes. This is an important point because, for example, a class can have an internal cache that changes on a call to a member function, but doesn't change the semantic state. Should that member function be `const` or not? Should it change when the implementation changes?

A C++ compiler sometimes needs to know this information. Also, it's important that you know this when placing objects in read-only memory (such as a shared area that only has read access), or when worrying about concurrency (acquiring a shared rather than exclusive lock). It's not reassuring to know that the semantic state is unchanged if you get a bus error, or worse, a subtle race condition.

You can solve the concurrency issue by protecting the object internally with a semaphore, but you really cannot solve the read-only memory problem. However, there are some workarounds you can use:

You can have both `const` **and non-`const` versions of the same function.** Because the C++ function overloading mechanism is sensitive to the `const` nature of member functions, the compiler uses one for a `const` object, and the other for a non-`const` object. This allows the non-`const` version to change the cache, while the `const` version cannot. The only problems are the usual ones for overloading, such as the way it interacts with overriding (see "Issues in overloading and overriding classes" on page 106). Also, there is less benefit for things like caching when you use `const`. This overloading applies to function arguments as well.

Use an accessor object (a type of surrogate, see page 95) to get the performance benefits of a cache and not change the object. Any modifiable state (like a cache) goes in the surrogate object—which might need to be a friend of the object to which it refers. The collection TIterators are an example of accessor objects— they are modified as you iterate, but the underlying collection is unchanged.

⊘ NOTE   This technique is also useful for general concurrency issues, as it sometimes removes the need for synchronization. For example, iterators from several different threads can freely access a collection that does not change.

If you must modify an object inside a `const` **member function,** cast the `this` pointer to a non-`const` pointer or declare the member in question as `mutable` (a new ANSI feature not yet added to many C++ compilers). If you do this, however, you must document that the function may not be called for an object in read-only memory, and you must either protect the object's state with an internal semaphore, or document that the function modifies the object internally (for example, it's not multithread safe). Taligent engineers must check with an architect first.

Static destructors for subsystem cleanup

Using destructors for static objects is the only way to ensure that a subsystem in a shared library performs some kind of cleanup at application quit time. Any static object destructor in your library can take care of finalization.

Because tasks don't always quit cleanly, you can't depend on shared library code to clean up resources used by the whole system; if the task quits unexpectedly, the resources do not get cleaned up. For those cases, have a server that manages the resources. You can use the connection capabilities of PROSE (part of the Message Streams library) and the Remote Object framework to track clients who die. If the client terminates normally, the normal cleanup can happen; but if the task disappears, the server must clean up all resources used by that task.

MISCELLANEOUS PROGRAMMING TIPS

Here is a collection of miscellaneous programming tips.

Create objects in a valid state

Construct objects in a valid, ready-to-use state, with all public member functions ready to do something sensible. Don't create objects in an invalid state and then expect the client to call an open routine, or to call a close routine before destruction.

Always allocate needed resources in the constructor because it is more convenient, and they are properly freed by the destructor if an exception occurs and the object is destroyed in a stack unwind.

✅ NOTE   There are only two exceptions to this rule. One is the virtual Initialize(). (For more information about Initialize(), see "Base class constructors cannot call virtual functions" on page 68.) The other exception is that a constructor may make an invalid object to be streamed into, but it must still be valid enough for the destructor to run.

Use flattening rather than dynamic class instantiation

If you need to dynamically instantiate a class, you will find it's usually easier to do so by using Taligent's Resurrect to unflatten a flattened polymorphic object. This is much easier than using the general interface for dynamically instantiating a class (especially as the latter doesn't currently exist in the Taligent Application Environment).

When the dynamic instantiation interface is there, go ahead and use it. Unflattening a flattened object is just much easier. In some cases, you might need the full interface, but definitely think about unflattening an object first.

Check for self-assignment with `operator =:`

A common mistake when implementing an assignment is to forget to check for self-references (the `this` pointer being the same as the argument being assigned). Clients will not normally do this intentionally, but it can happen accidentally, and with aliasing you cannot always tell when it's going to happen. It can also happen to surrogates, where the surrogate being assigned points at the same master object as the target of the assignment.

To avoid self-assignment, do nothing if `this` and the assignment argument are the same; but, if the argument is a reference, take its address. Also, make sure you do things in the right order: for example, when reference counting, increment the count of the new master before decrementing the count of the old master.

Balance overloaded operators

Include overloaded operators in balanced sets; for example, if you define ==, then define !=.

Use static members as constructors

When the standard constructor mechanism is too inflexible, you can use a static member function that calls a private constructor to create a partially valid object, then finishes building it, and returns the result.

Static member constructors are useful because they can have different names, and you can force an object to be on the heap by making all constructors private. The disadvantage is that if you want the object to work both heap allocated and non-heap allocated, you need two versions of the static function, and the nonheap version must copy the object.

This technique can be useful occasionally, but use it sparingly.

Differentiate overloaded constructors

Sometimes you want to overload constructors, but discover that the argument types you want to use are not sufficient to differentiate those constructors. A good solution is to use a lightweight (inline) nested class to wrap constructor arguments in a distinct type that's easy to overload. For example, in the Graphics system, one early design for TGrafMatrix had constructors that were similar to:

```
TGrafMatrix(const Translate &);
TGrafMatrix(const Rotate &);
TGrafMatrix(const Scale &);
```

The three argument types are nested classes whose constructors take appropriate arguments. A call to create a translation matrix looks like this:

```
TGrafMatrix(TGrafMatrix::Translate(point));
```

Eventually, with name spaces, the helper classes might not have to be nested, which will make this kind of construct easier to type.

Hide implementation classes

Classes that are used solely by your implementation needn't be declared in your public header file, as long as your class refers to them by pointer or reference. You only need a partial declaration, like this:

```
class TImplementation;
```

This suffices as long as you don't embed such an object, create one, or access any of its members outside of your private implementation.

Use nil pointer deletion

C++ defines `delete p`, where p is a nil pointer, to be a valid operation (nothing happens). This can be very useful, especially in exception handlers.

Issues in overloading and overriding classes

If you override an overloaded member function (virtual or not), your override hides all overloaded variants of that member function, *not just the one you overrode.* To properly override an overloaded member function, you must override all the overloaded variants. Of course, the overriding function can turn around and call the one from the base class.

In the following example, bar.Foo(2) calls B::Foo(double) after coercing the int argument to double. This is because the override of Foo(double) introduces the name Foo in B's scope, hiding that name from A's scope; again, the rule is that all overloaded variants constitute one name that is hidden or not.

```
class A {
public:
    void Foo(long);
    void Foo(double);
};

class B: public A {
public:
    void Foo(double);                // Override hides Foo(long)
};

B bar;
bar.Foo(2);                          // Coerced to double
```

However, a call to an A object goes to A::Foo(long) because the override in B hides Foo(long) only in B's name scope, not in A's.

```
A& br = bar;
br.Foo(2);                           // Calls A::Foo(long)
```

✓ NOTE   The Taligent C++ Compiler warns you if you override some but not all of a set of overloaded virtual member functions.

Overridden, overloaded functions are single entities

C++ treats an overloaded function as a single entity because the C++ scope resolution rule is to find the first class containing any function that defines that name, then to look for a match based on argument type. The C++ design team believes this is the correct rule; their reasoning is that an overloaded set of functions is really just one function with several variants, and you should not name functions with the same name unless they are really the same function.

Control class access

Assign `private` and `protected` to special member functions to control access and use of your class.

Type of control	Controlled by making...
Only derived classes can call them	Some constructors `protected`
The object cannot be copied	Assignment and copy constructor `private`
Only derived classes can copy the object	Assignment and copy constructor `protected`
Clients cannot delete the object directly or allocate it on the stack	Destructors `private` or `protected`
Client cannot allocate object on the heap	Operator `new` `private` or `protected`

Remember, C++ has access control, not visibility control, so making something private means it's still defined, but some clients can't use it.

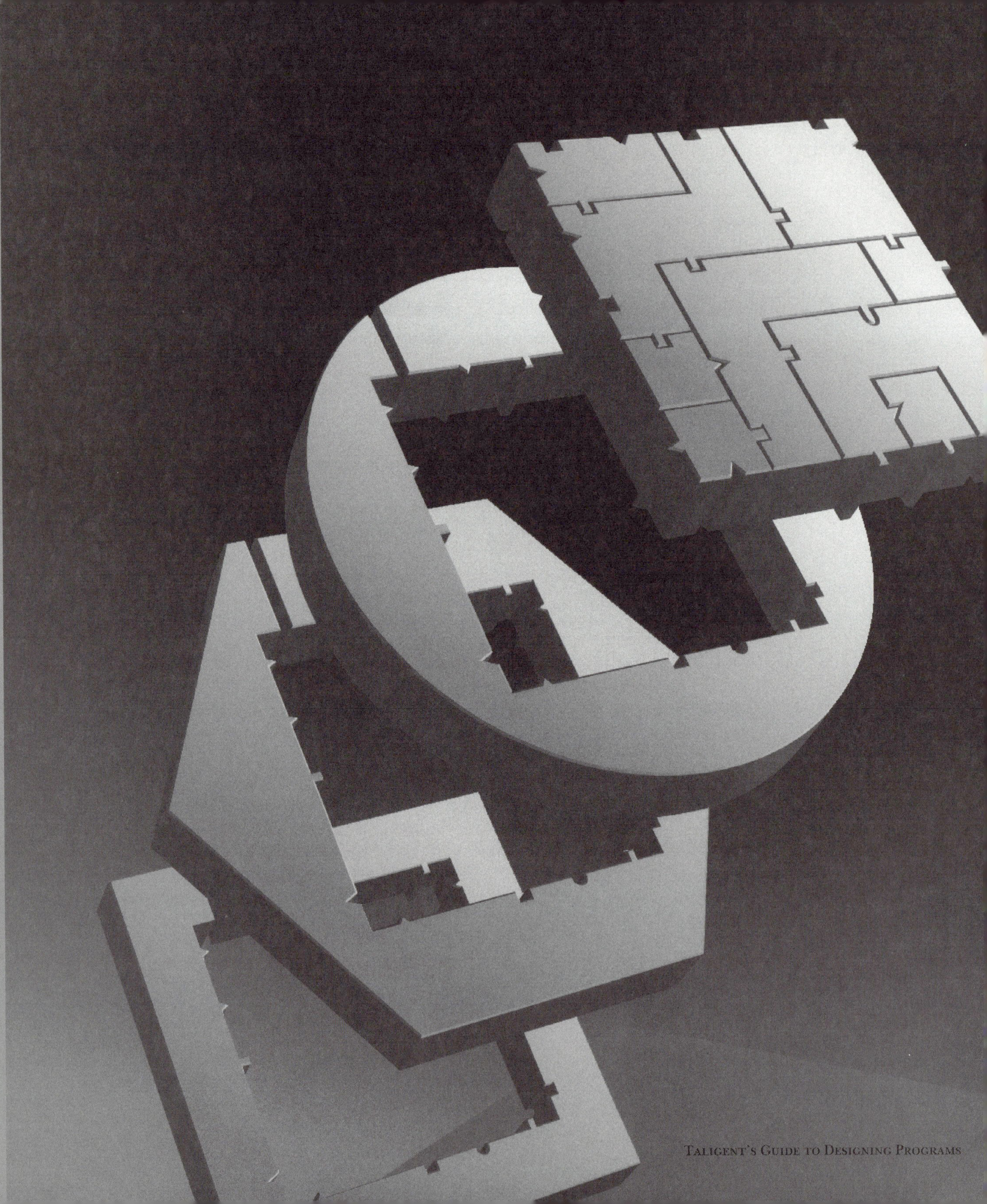

Taligent's Guide to Designing Programs

CHAPTER 6

PORTABILITY ISSUES

One important goal for the Taligent Application Environment is portability to a wide variety of processor architectures. Experience shows that achieving portability takes diligence and hard work. As you develop your application, be careful not to leave traps that will cause your code to stumble when it moves to another platform. This chapter contains some important rules for achieving a smooth transition between platforms.

LANGUAGE AND HARDWARE ASSUMPTIONS

To write portable code, avoid assumptions about the language or hardware. Assumptions tend to lurk behind the scenes and then leap into the spotlight at inopportune moments.

Safe assumptions

There are few safe assumptions that you can make about raw C and C++ data types, and these are *all you can safely assume*:

- `char` is guaranteed to hold only 0 to 127, and can be either unsigned or signed `char`; you cannot assume one or the other. Avoid `char` unless you do not care about sign extension.
- `unsigned char` can hold from 0 to 255; it can hold more.
- `signed char` can hold from –127 to +127; it can hold more.
- `short` can hold from –32,767 to 32,767 (signed) or 0 to 65,535 (unsigned).

- int can hold from –32,767 to 32,767 (signed) or 0 to 65,535 (unsigned). *Ints cannot be counted on to hold any more than a short.* If you need something larger than a short, use a long. If a short is big enough, use int instead to improve efficiency by taking advantage of a processor's natural word size.

  Always read and write an int by casting it to a short, because that's all you're guaranteed to get.

  The Taligent stream classes do not read or write int because int doesn't have a portable representation.

- long can hold from –2,147,483,647 to 2,147,483,647 (signed) or 0 to 4,294,967,295 (unsigned).

- float is a IEEE single-precision number and double is a IEEE double-precision number. This is because the Taligent Application Environment runs only on processors that support the IEEE floating point standard and that support the single- and double-precision types.

On some machines, a 32-bit operation is more efficient than a 16-bit operation because there is no need to do masking.

If you need exact information about a raw data type, use the symbols defined in limits.h and float.h. However, remember that the values of these symbols can change from processor to processor or compiler to compiler, within the limits defined above (for more information, see the ANSI/ISO C specification).

In general, watch your assumptions carefully, and use typedefs instead of C types. For examples, see "Avoid raw C types with dimensions" on page 40.

Bad assumptions

Bad assumptions make your code nonportable. For example, don't assume that:

- int and long are the same size; these can vary between processors
- long, float, double, or long double can be at any even address
- You know the memory layout of a data type, including its byte order
- You know how a struct or class is laid out in memory, or that it can be written to or read from a data file as a memory image
- You know the alignment restrictions or sizes for data types
- You know how the calling conventions are implemented, or indeed any detail of the language implementation or runtime. For example, some architectures pass arguments on the stack, others in registers.

Additionally, here are a few points to remember when writing your program:

Pointers and integers are not interchangeable. Neither is guaranteed to hold the other.

Use `void*` **if you want an untyped pointer,** not `char*`. Pointer arithmetic can't be done using `void*` pointers; instead, use a typed pointer (`char*` for bytes).

Long double is an inherently nonportable data type and can vary in size and precision from processor to processor. It is guaranteed to hold any number a `float` or `double` can hold, but that's about all you can count on (for example, many RISC processors don't support any IEEE extended-precision format). Therefore, `long double` is suitable only for in-memory computations, not for data storage or network transmission. What's more, a `long double` is sometimes implemented in software and is therefore slower on some platforms.

Don't make assumptions about memory alignment because of variations between processors and compilers. Here are some common problems with alignment:

■ 68020 processors and later allow access to any primitive data type without alignment restrictions (such as when a `void*` or `char*` pointer is cast to a longer data type). Because most RISC processors don't support this kind of access, code that assumes the lack of restriction is not portable.

■ Most RISC processors require that 4-byte quantities (`long`, `float`) be on a 4-byte boundary and that 8-byte quantities (`double`) be on an 8-byte boundary. The compiler forces this alignment on structure elements, but if you make assumptions, you can get structures with lots of unused space.

■ Some compilers, such as MPW™ C, let you have long elements of a `struct` or `class` on a 2-byte boundary. This is inefficient on 68020 and later processors, because the placement requires two memory accesses rather than one.

⊘ NOTE   Avoid problems like this by ordering the data members in descending order of size to minimize alignment problems (both space and speed) on most architectures.

Processor portability

To illustrate portability problems, consider the MIPS R4000. This processor has 64-bit integers and 64-bit pointers.

Future PowerPC chips will also support 64 bits. However, it's not clear whether a C compiler will make `long` or `int` 64 bits.

Other machines can also have large pointers (theoretically up to 48 bits on the 80386) but with 32-bit integers.

SYNCHRONIZATION

Do not use synchronization outside the scope of the supported synchronization constructs (such as semaphores, monitors, and Taligent's MReferenceCounted). Rapid changes in hardware designs make all such constructs potentially unsafe and nonportable. For example, on both the PowerPC™ and Alpha architectures, reads and writes can appear to happen in different orders to different processors within a multiprocessor.

At Taligent, there are no exceptions unless specifically granted by an architect.

PORTABLE DATA

The Taligent Application Environment runs on different processors—sometimes concurrently. If you write or read any data in a context where it might go to or come from a different CPU running the Taligent Application Environment, you have to worry about formats. Such situations include reading or writing disk files, or sending IPC messages that go over a network (or even over an expansion bus). The other CPU might even have a different byte order!

A solution to this problem is to pick a canonical format for messages and data files that is the same no matter what the CPU. The Taligent Application Environment package for reading and writing objects (TStream) already does this. TStream also has static member functions you can call to convert to and from this canonical format without using a stream.

Just because you have a canonical format doesn't mean you must pay a big overhead every time you access your data. One alternative is to perform the translation to or from the canonical format at a predetermined time. For example, TrueType outline fonts have a certain canonical format that depends heavily on the 680x0 architecture. However, you could convert them to a convenient local format when they are installed or when they are used, rather than accessing them directly in their canonical format.

Some data types aren't portable:

- Certain data types can't be written to be portable to disk or on a network. These include `int`, `long double`, and any pointer or pointer to member.
- Many standard types, such as ANSI's `size_t` and `ptrdiff_t`, have definitions that vary between CPUs.
- Some objects (such as TThreadHandle) have no meaning when written to disk or over the network; they are valid only during one session on one system. Such objects signal an exception in their flatten and unflatten operators when the TStream has the kDeepFreeze attribute. (A kDeepFreeze attribute of the stream is set if the flattening should store the object in its most general form—that is, a form that can be resurrected on another CPU or saved to disk and resurrected.)

ASSEMBLY LANGUAGE

Do not use assembly language. It isn't portable and must be rewritten for every processor that the Taligent Application Environment runs on. Taligent does not allow use of assembly language except where specifically approved in advance by an architect.

NONPORTABLE CODE

If you have to write nonportable code, take the following steps (a Taligent engineer must first clear it with an architect):

1 Clearly mark the code with a comment indicating it is nonportable.

```
//??? NOT PORTABLE
```

It is then easy to find such constructs with a global search.

2 Identify the environment for which the code is specific.

✅ NOTE   Contact Taligent for detailed guidelines.

3 Include the name of the processor family somewhere in the filename, such as `FooClassRS6000.C`, if the entire file is processor dependent.

Appendix A

Class templates

Template implementations are hard to maintain because they get compiled into your client's code. Templates also, by their very nature, tend to bloat the resulting object code. This guide provides design standards and conventions to increase code maintainability, and to reduce the memory footprint.

There are many possible designs for template; some are easier to write, while others share more of the implementation details. The best design depends upon the specifics of your code. This guide recommends a standard design, but also gives some alternatives for special circumstances.

Definitions and conventions

The nomenclature of templates is confusing. According to the ANSI drafts, a *class template* is the definition of the template for the class.

```
template <class AType>
class TArrayOf {...} ;
```

A *specialized class* is a class produced by invoking the template.

```
TArrayOf<TGPoint> array;
```

Template conventions

By convention, class template names end in prepositions. Choose the preposition that makes the most sense when you describe the specialized class in English:

- TArrayOf<TGPoint> is an array *of* TGPoints.
- TCommandOn<TGPoint> is a command *on* a TGPoint reference.
- TFunnelFor<TFile> is a passive iterator *for* TFile objects.

In class template declarations, begin the type-argument type-id with a capital *A*:

```
template<class AType>
class TArrayOf ... ;
```

**Include file
conventions**

The implementation of your noninline class template methods should be hidden from your clients. Unfortunately, many C++ compilers require that the source of the noninline class template methods implementation be available at the client's compile time. To keep the noninline class template method implementations from cluttering your include file, place them in a separate include file, and #include the separate include file at the end of the regular include file.

If your include file is MyFile.h, name the implementation include file *MyFileTemplateMethods.h.* (The filename should be *MyFileTemplateMethods.C;* but the current build tools require header files to end in .h.)

MyFile.h ——————

```
#ifndef Taligent_MYFILE
#define Taligent_MYFILE

template <class AType>
class TMyTemplate { ... };

#ifndef Taligent_MYFILETEMPLATEMETHODS
#include <MyFileTemplateMethods.h>
#endif

#endif
```

MyFileTemplateMethods.h ——
*contains noninline
class template method
implementations*

```
#ifndef Taligent_MYFILETEMPLATEMETHODS
#define Taligent_MYFILETEMPLATEMETHODS

#ifndef Taligent_MYFILE
#include <MyFile.h>
#endif

template <class AType>
TMyTemplate::TMyTemplate() { ... }

#endif
```

SHARING CLASS TEMPLATE IMPLEMENTATIONS

Any implementation-sharing class template design has to answer the following questions:

- How does the class template delegate to the implementation class?
- How does the implementation class perform type-specific operations?

The best design, however, depends upon the specifics of your code.

General rules for implementation classes

To be reusable, the implementation class deals with objects at the level common to all types that your template can be instantiated with. For maximum reuse, your implementation should be `void`; for rare cases it can be a more specific type. For polymorphism, refer to the objects using pointers (`void*`) .

✅ NOTE   Because it is contrary to the normal style rules, you should not use a pointer to pass an argument to a method that is not going to alias or own the argument. But, because `void&` is illegal in C++, you must use `void*` in all such cases—even though the method is not going to alias or own the argument.

An implementation class does not have enough information to perform type-specific operations, so it delegates these operations to a specialized class. The specialized class' methods cast the `void*` arguments back to the correct type and perform the type-specific operation. Because these casts are blind casts, the object must always be cast to and from the same type. If you pass in the object as a base class, but extract it as a derived class, the C++ compiler will not perform the pointer fix-up, and you will end up with an incorrect pointer value.

```
class TBase { ... };
class TDerived : public TBase, virtual public VVirtual { ... };
void FunctionTakingTBaseAsVoid(void* item);

void f()
{
    TBase base;
    TDerived derived;
    FunctionTakingTBaseAsVoid(item);                    // Correct
    FunctionTakingTBaseAsVoid(d&erived);                // Incorrect
    FunctionTakingTBaseAsVoid((TBase*) &derived);       // Correct
}

void FunctionTakingTBaseAsVoid(void* item)
{
    TBase* asBase = (TBase*) item;                      // Correct
    TDerived* asDerived = (TDerived*) item;             // Incorrect
    TDerived* asDerived = (TDerived*) (TBase*) item;    // Correct, conditionally
}
```

Correct only if you somehow know the item is a TDerived (Not a great design)

The C++ compiler catches most attempts to perform type-specific operations on void objects; however, the delete operator is the one exception. Deleting a pointer to an object that is held as a void* silently releases the storage that the object occupies, but does not call that object's destructor.

```
{
    void* baseAsVoid = new TBase(...);

    delete baseAsVoid;                   // Incorrect. Destructor not called.
    TBase* base = (TBase*) baseAsVoid;
    delete base;                         // Correct
}
```

THE EXAMPLE CLASS: AN OWNING STACK

The remainder of this guide uses an *owning stack* to illustrate the various template techniques. The example uses a stack because it is simple to implement. The owning feature forces the examples to deal with type-specific copy and delete operations. To make the examples short, there is no error checking.

Here is the owning stack as an ordinary, nonspecialized class:

Example1.h

```
// Copyright (C)1994 Taligent, Inc. All rights reserved.
// $Revision: $
#ifndef Taligent_EXAMPLE1
#define Taligent_EXAMPLE1

class TCollectibleLong;

class TOwningStackOf1
{
public:
            TOwningStackOf1();
            TOwningStackOf1( const TOwningStackOf1& other );
    virtual ~TOwningStackOf1();
            // Operator= omitted. It's like the copy constructor.

    virtual void Adopt( TCollectibleLong* item );
            // Orphan omitted. It's like Adopt.

    virtual unsigned int    Count() const;
private:
    TCollectibleLong*       fStack[10];
    unsigned int            fount;
};

#endif
```

ExampleImplementation.C —

```
// Copyright (C)1994 Taligent, Inc. All rights reserved.
// $Revision: $
#ifndef Taligent_EXAMPLE1
#include <Example1.h>
#endif

#ifndef Taligent_CLASSICDATASTRUCTURES
#include <ClassicDataStructures.h>
#endif

TOwningStackOf1::TOwningStackOf1()
    : fCount(0)
{
}

TOwningStackOf1::TOwningStackOf1(
    const TOwningStackOf1& other)
    : fCount(other.fCount)
{
    for ( unsigned int i = 0; i < fCount; i++ )
    {
        fStack[i] = new TCollectibleLong(*other.fStack[i]);
    }
}

TOwningStackOf1::~TOwningStackOf1()
{
    for ( unsigned int i = 0; i < fCount; i++ )
    {
        delete fStack[i];
    }
}

void TOwningStackOf1::Adopt( TCollectibleLong* item )
{
    fStack[fCount++] = item;
}

unsigned int TOwningStackOf1::Count() const
{
    return fCount;
}
```

To templatize the class without sharing the implementation:

Example2.h

```
// Copyright (C)1994 Taligent, Inc. All rights reserved.
// $Revision: $
#ifndef Taligent_EXAMPLE2
#define Taligent_EXAMPLE2

#ifndef Taligent_PRIMITIVECLASSES
#include <PrimitiveClasses.h>
#endif

template <class AType>
class TOwningStackOf2
{
public:
            TOwningStackOf2();
            TOwningStackOf2( const TOwningStackOf2<AType>& other );
    virtual ~TOwningStackOf2();
    virtual void Adopt( AType* item );
    virtual unsigned int Count() const;
private:
    AType*  fStack[10];
    unsigned int    fCount;
};

#ifndef Taligent_EXAMPLE2TEMPLATEIMPLEMENTATION
#include <Example2TemplateImplementation.h>
#endif

#endif
```

Example2Implementations.h

```
#ifndef Taligent_EXAMPLE2TEMPLATEIMPLEMENTATION
#define Taligent_EXAMPLE2TEMPLATEIMPLEMENTATION

#ifndef Taligent_EXAMPLE2
#include <Example2.h>
#endif

template<class AType>
TOwningStackOf2<AType>::TOwningStackOf2()
    : fCount(0)
{
}

template<class AType>
TOwningStackOf2<AType>::TOwningStackOf2( const TOwningStackOf2<AType>& other )
    : fCount(other.fCount)
{
    for ( unsigned int i = 0; i < fCount; i++ )
    {
        fStack[i] = new AType(*other.fStack[i]);
    }
}

template<class AType>
TOwningStackOf2<AType>::~TOwningStackOf2()
{
    for ( unsigned int i = 0; i < fCount; i++ )
    {
        delete fStack[i];
    }
}

template<class AType>
void TOwningStackOf2<AType>::Adopt( AType* item )
{
    fStack[fCount++] = item;
}

template<class AType>
unsigned int TOwningStackOf2<AType>::Count() const
{
    return fCount;
}

#endif
```

SHARING THE IMPLEMENTATION THROUGH PRIVATE INHERITANCE

This technique uses private inheritance to share the implementation class between multiple specializations of the template. For an alternate technique of holding the implementation class as a member variable, see "Sharing the implementation by delegating to a member" on page 130.

Class definitions

If your class template is TXXX, define two classes:

TXXXImplementation is a nontemplatized abstract base class that has methods for implementing the operations of the template. When the implementation methods need to perform a type-specific operation, they delegate to private pure virtual methods. The pure-virtual type-specific methods typically include deleting, copying, comparing, and streaming.

TXXX is a class template for a concrete class that privately inherits from TXXXImplementation. It has public methods that delegate to the TXXXImplementation implementation methods, and private virtual methods that implement the TXXXImplementation type-specific methods.

Naming conventions

Follow these three naming conventions:

For the implementation class, if your class template is *TFoo*, the private implementation class should be *TFooImplementation*.

For the implementation methods, if an implementation method does not have a type-specific signature (it does not have AType in its argument list), name it the same as the public template method, and reexport it by using the qualified name in the class declaration. Otherwise, change the name to prevent the compiler from generating warnings. If your template method is *Bar*, the implementation method should be *ImplementBar*.

For the type-specific methods, if your type-specific operation is *IsEqual*, the type-specific method should be *TypeSpecificIsEqual*.

Instance variables

Place both type-specific and non-type-specific instance variables in the implementation class. Treat *non*-type-specific instance variables normally, and use their real type. For type-specific instance variables, hold them by a pointer to the most derived common base type, which is usually `void`.

Type-specific methods and implementation class constructors and destructors

Type-specific methods are virtual methods. You cannot call them from the implementation class' constructors or destructors, because they will not be defined when the implementation class' constructor runs.

To perform type-specific operations at construction time, add a separate ImplementConstructor method to the implementation class. Call it from the class template's constructor, after the implementation class is constructed.

To perform type-specific operations at destruction time, add an ImplementDestructor method to the implementation called from the class template's destructor.

Here is the wrong way to implement the TOwningStackOf copy constructor:

```
template <class AType>
TOwningStackOf::TOwningStackOf(const TOwningStackOf<AType>& other)
    : TOwningStackOfImplementation(other)
{
}

TOwningStackOfImplementation::TOwningStackOfImplementation(
    const TOwningStackOfImplementation& other)
    : fCount(other.fCount)
{
    for ( unsigned int i = 0; i < fCount; i++ )
    {
        fStack[i] = TypeSpecificCopy(other.fStack[i]);
    }
}
```

Fails—TypeSpecificCopy is virtual and cannot be called from a constructor

Here is the correct way:

```
TOwningStackOf::TOwningStackOf(const TOwningStackOf<AType>& other)
{
    ImplementConstructor(other);
}

void TOwningStackOfImplementation::ImplementConstructor(
    const TOwningStackOfImplementation& other)
{
    fCount = other.fCount;
    for ( unsigned int i = 0; i < fCount; i++ )
    {
        fStack[i] = TypeSpecificCopy(other.fStack[i]);
    }
}
```

Inlining the class template's public methods

The class template's methods do little more than delegate to the implementation class. Like all normal Taligent Application Environment methods, you should declare most of the class template's methods virtual. Additionally, make the implementations inline to avoid an extra method call where the class template is used nonpolymorphically.

Do not inline the class template's type-specific methods. The implementation class is the only client, and it will always call them polymorphically.

Class templates that inherit from specialized classes

You can use this technique with public inheritance from a templatized base class. If you do so, don't mix an implementation class into any of the public base class. Defer all the implementation to the derived classes to avoid the diamond inheritance problem. See "Be aware of problems with virtual bases" on page 18.

An implementation sharing example

Putting all of these rules together, here's the owning stack implemented with private inheritance for implementation sharing.

Example3.h

```
// Copyright (C)1994 Taligent, Inc. All rights reserved.
// $Revision: $

#ifndef Taligent_EXAMPLE3
#define Taligent_EXAMPLE3

#ifndef Taligent_PRIMITIVECLASSES
#include <PrimitiveClasses.h>
#endif

class TOwningStackOf3Implementation
{
public:
            TOwningStackOf3Implementation();
    virtual ~TOwningStackOf3Implementation();
    void    ImplementConstructor( const TOwningStackOf3Implementation& other );
    void    ImplementDestructor();
    void    ImplementAdopt(void* item);
    virtual unsigned int    Count() const;
private:
    virtual void *  TypeSpecificCopy(const void* item) = 0;
    virtual void    TypeSpecificDelete(void* item) = 0;
    void*           fStack[10];
    unsigned int    fCount;
};
```

Example3.h

```
template <class AType>
class TOwningStackOf3
      : private TOwningStackOf3Implementation
{
public:
            TOwningStackOf3();
            TOwningStackOf3( const TOwningStackOf3<AType>& other );
    virtual ~TOwningStackOf3();
    virtual void    Adopt(AType* graphic);
            // Reexport Count
            TOwningStackOf3Implementation::Count;
private:
    virtual void *  TypeSpecificCopy(const void* item);
    virtual void    TypeSpecificDelete(void* item);
};

#ifndef Taligent_EXAMPLE3TEMPLATEIMPLEMENTATION
#include <Example3TemplateImplementation.h>
#endif

// Inlines go here

template<class AType>
inline
TOwningStackOf3<AType>::TOwningStackOf3()
{
}

template<class AType>
inline
TOwningStackOf3<AType>::TOwningStackOf3( const TOwningStackOf3<AType>& other )
{
    ImplementConstructor(other);
}

template<class AType>
inline
TOwningStackOf3<AType>::~TOwningStackOf3()
{
    ImplementDestructor();
}

template<class AType>
inline
void TOwningStackOf3<AType>::Adopt(AType* item)
{
    ImplementAdopt(item);
}
```

Example3Implementation.C —

```
// Copyright (C) 1994 Taligent, Inc. All rights reserved.
// $Revision: $

#ifndef Taligent_EXAMPLE3
#include <Example3.h>
#endif

TOwningStackOf3Implementation::TOwningStackOf3Implementation()
    : fCount(0)
{
}

TOwningStackOf3Implementation::~TOwningStackOf3Implementation()
{
}

void TOwningStackOf3Implementation::ImplementConstructor(
    const TOwningStackOf3Implementation& other)
{
    fCount = other.fCount;
    for ( unsigned int i = 0; i < fCount; i++ )
    {
        fStack[i] = TypeSpecificCopy(other.fStack[i]);
    }
}

void TOwningStackOf3Implementation::ImplementDestructor()
{
    for ( unsigned int i = 0; i < fCount; i++ )
    {
        TypeSpecificDelete(fStack[i]);
    }
}

void TOwningStackOf3Implementation::ImplementAdopt(void* item)
{
    fStack[fCount++] = item;
}

unsigned int TOwningStackOf3Implementation::Count() const
{
    return fCount;
}
```

Example3Implementation.h —

```
// Copyright (C)1994 Taligent, Inc. All rights reserved.
// $Revision: $

#ifndef Taligent_EXAMPLE3TEMPLATEIMPLEMENTATION
#define Taligent_EXAMPLE3TEMPLATEIMPLEMENTATION

#ifndef Taligent_EXAMPLE3
#include <Example3.h>
#endif

template<class AType>
void* TOwningStackOf3<AType>::TypeSpecificCopy(const void* item)
{
    return new AType(* (const AType*) item);
}

template<class AType>
void TOwningStackOf3<AType>::TypeSpecificDelete(void* item)
{
    delete (AType*) item;
}

#endif
```

Example3TemplateMethods.C

```cpp
// Copyright (C)1994 Taligent, Inc. All rights reserved.
// $Revision: $

#ifndef Taligent_EXAMPLE3
#include <Example3.h>
#endif

TOwningStackOf3Implementation::TOwningStackOf3Implementation()
    : fCount(0)
{
}


TOwningStackOf3Implementation::~TOwningStackOf3Implementation()
{
}

void TOwningStackOf3Implementation::ImplementConstructor(
    const TOwningStackOf3Implementation& other)
{
    fCount = other.fCount;
    for ( unsigned int i = 0; i < fCount; i++ )
    {
        fStack[i] = TypeSpecificCopy(other.fStack[i]);
    }
}

void TOwningStackOf3Implementation::ImplementDestructor()
{
    for ( unsigned int i = 0; i < fCount; i++ )
    {
        TypeSpecificDelete(fStack[i]);
    }
}

void TOwningStackOf3Implementation::ImplementAdopt(void* item)
{
    fStack[fCount++] = item;
}

unsigned int TOwningStackOf3Implementation::Count() const
{
    return fCount;
}
```

SHARING THE IMPLEMENTATION BY DELEGATING TO A MEMBER

An alterative to private inheritance is to delegate the implementation to a member. This technique usually leads to cleaner code than achieved by using private inheritance.

No matter which implementation sharing technique you choose, you must still connect the implementation class with the type-specific operations. There are several ways to achieve this:

The implementation defines pure virtual functions for the type-specific operations. These are overridden by a derived class template. (This is what is done in the private inheritance case.)

The implementation is given a pointer or reference to an object which has virtual methods for the type-specific operation. (This is what happens in the following example.)

The implementation is given a set of pointer-to-member functions to the type-specific operations.

An example of delegating to a member

The following is an example of a class template that delegates the implementation to a member. It has two main features:

The type-specific protocol is encapsulated in a small standalone abstract base class; public class template creates concrete instances.

The public class template has an implementation class as a member, which has a pointer to the type-specific protocol class.

While there are more classes involved, and more delegation, this design is cleaner than the private implementation example on page 125. Because the type-specific class is passed into the implementation class, the implementation class constructors and destructors are free to use the type-specific operators. So there is no need to treat construction or destruction specially.

The delegation example's naming conventions

For this technique, if TXXX is the class template, the naming conventions are:

TXXX is the class template.

TXXXImplementation is the implementation.

TXXXTypeSpecificOperationsBase is the abstract base of the type-specific operations.

TXXXTypeSpecificOperations is the class template for the type-specific operations.

Because there is no inheritance between the class template and the implementation class, there is no chance of a name collision. In this way, the method names of the implementation classes don't require a special prefix.

The delegating-to-a-member example

Example4.h

```
// Copyright (C)1994 Taligent, Inc. All rights reserved.
// $Revision: $

#ifndef Taligent_EXAMPLE4
#define Taligent_EXAMPLE4

#ifndef Taligent_PRIMITIVECLASSES
#include <PrimitiveClasses.h>
#endif

class TOwningStackOf4TypeSpecificOperationsBase;

class TOwningStackOf4Implementation
{
public:
            TOwningStackOf4Implementation(
                TOwningStackOf4TypeSpecificOperationsBase* adopt);

            TOwningStackOf4Implementation(
                TOwningStackOf4TypeSpecificOperationsBase* adopt,
                const TOwningStackOf4Implementation& other);

    virtual ~TOwningStackOf4Implementation();
    virtual void     Adopt(void* item);
    virtual unsigned int    Count() const;
private:
    TOwningStackOf4TypeSpecificOperationsBase* fTypeSpecificOperations;
    unsigned int     fCount;
    void*            fStack[10];
};

template <class AType>
class TOwningStackOf4
{
public:
            TOwningStackOf4();
            TOwningStackOf4( const TOwningStackOf4<AType>& other );
    virtual ~TOwningStackOf4();
    virtual void     Adopt(AType* graphic);
    virtual unsigned int    Count() const;
private:
    TOwningStackOf4ImplementationfImplementation;
};

#ifndef Taligent_EXAMPLE4TEMPLATEIMPLEMENTATION
#include <Example4TemplateImplementation.h>
#endif

// Inlines go here
```

Example4.h

```
template<class AType>
inline
TOwningStackOf4<AType>::TOwningStackOf4()
    : fImplementation(new TOwningStackOf4TypeSpecificOperations<AType>)
{
}

template<class AType>
inline
TOwningStackOf4<AType>::TOwningStackOf4( const TOwningStackOf4<AType>& other )
    : fImplementation(new TOwningStackOf4TypeSpecificOperations<AType>,
        other.fImplementation)
{
}

template<class AType>
inline
TOwningStackOf4<AType>::~TOwningStackOf4()
{
}

template<class AType>
inline
void TOwningStackOf4<AType>::Adopt(AType* item)
{
    fImplementation.Adopt(item);
}

template<class AType>
inline
unsigned int TOwningStackOf4<AType>::Count() const
{
    return fImplementation.Count();
}

template<class AType>
inline
TOwningStackOf4TypeSpecificOperations<AType>::TOwningStackOf4TypeSpecificOperations()
{
}

#endif
```

Example4Implementation.h —

```
// Copyright (C) 1994 Taligent, Inc. All rights reserved.
// $Revision: $

#ifndef Taligent_EXAMPLE4TEMPLATEIMPLEMENTATION
#define Taligent_EXAMPLE4TEMPLATEIMPLEMENTATION

#ifndef Taligent_EXAMPLE4
#include <Example4.h>
#endif

class TOwningStackOf4TypeSpecificOperationsBase
{
public:
                TOwningStackOf4TypeSpecificOperationsBase() {};
    virtual     ~TOwningStackOf4TypeSpecificOperationsBase() {};
    virtual void *  Copy(const void* item) = 0;
    virtual void    Delete(void* item) = 0;
};

template<class AType>
class TOwningStackOf4TypeSpecificOperations
    : public  TOwningStackOf4TypeSpecificOperationsBase
{
public:
            TOwningStackOf4TypeSpecificOperations();
    virtual void *  Copy(const void* item);
    virtual void    Delete(void* item);
};

template<class AType>
void*
TOwningStackOf4TypeSpecificOperations<AType>::Copy(const void* item)
{
    return new AType(* (const AType*) item);
}

template<class AType>
void
TOwningStackOf4TypeSpecificOperations<AType>::Delete(void* item)
{
    delete (AType*) item;
}

#endif
```

Example4Implementation.C

```
// Copyright (C) 1994 Taligent, Inc. All rights reserved.
// $Revision: $

#ifndef Taligent_EXAMPLE4
#include <Example4.h>
#endif

// Methods of TOwningStackOf4Implementation
TOwningStackOf4Implementation::TOwningStackOf4Implementation(
                TOwningStackOf4TypeSpecificOperationsBase* adopt )
    : fTypeSpecificOperations(adopt), fCount(0)
{
}


TOwningStackOf4Implementation::TOwningStackOf4Implementation(
                TOwningStackOf4TypeSpecificOperationsBase* adopt,
                    const TOwningStackOf4Implementation& other)
    : fTypeSpecificOperations(adopt), fCount(other.fCount)
{
    for ( unsigned int i = 0; i < fCount; i++ )
    {
        fStack[i] = fTypeSpecificOperations->Copy(other.fStack[i]);
    }
}


TOwningStackOf4Implementation::~TOwningStackOf4Implementation()
{
    for ( unsigned int i = 0; i < fCount; i++ )
    {
        fTypeSpecificOperations->Delete(fStack[i]);
    }
    delete fTypeSpecificOperations;
}


void TOwningStackOf4Implementation::Adopt(void* item)
{
    fStack[fCount++] = item;
}


unsigned int TOwningStackOf4Implementation::Count() const
{
    return fCount;
}
```

FURTHER READING

For more information about templates, see:

- *Advanced C++ Programming Styles and Idioms* (Coplien), §7.4.
- *Working Paper for Draft Proposed American International Standard for Information Systems—Programming Language C++*, §14.
- *The C++ Programming Language, Second Edition* (Stroustrup), Chapter 8.

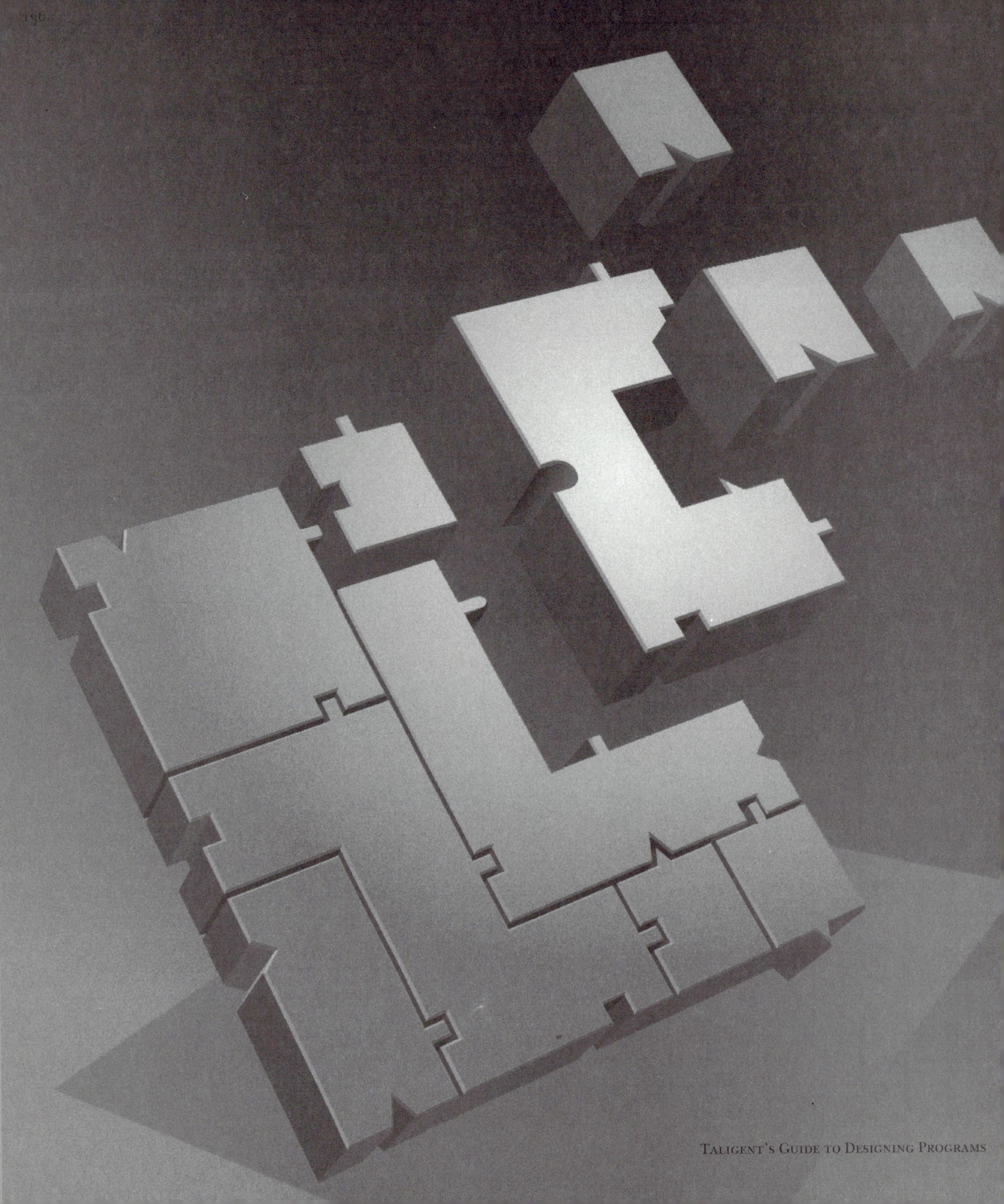

BIBLIOGRAPHY

Bentley, Jon. *Programming Pearls*. Reading, MA: Addison-Wesley, 1989.

———. *More Programming Pearls*. Reading, MA: Addison-Wesley, 1988.

———. *Writing Efficient Programs*. Englewood Cliffs, NJ: Prentice-Hall, 1982.

Booch, Grady. *Object Oriented Design with Applications*. 2d ed. Redwood City, CA: Benjamin/Cummings, 1994. This is one of the best books on object-oriented design. Mr. Booch thoroughly covers the ins and outs of it. If you read nothing else, read this book.

Cargill, Tom. *C++ Programming Style*. Reading, MA: Addison-Wesley, 1992. This book contains that rare and useful information—examples of bad code with analyses. Like the original *Elements of Programming Style*, this book is quite helpful because it shows what not to do.

Carroll, Martin. "Design of the USL Standard Components." *C++ Report* 5, no. 5 (June 1993).

Coplien, James O. *Advanced C++ Programming Styles and Idioms*. Reading, MA: Addison-Wesley, 1992. Lots and lots of useful techniques. However, it can be fairly dense at points, it isn't well organized, and some of the examples run counter to rules in this and other books.

Ellis, Margaret, and Bjarne Stroustrup. *The Annotated C++ Reference Manual*. Reading, MA: Addison-Wesley, 1990. This book has been supplanted by the current working paper for the draft ANSI C++ standard. It reflects the state of the language at the start of the standardization process a few years ago. Neither this book (abbreviated as the ARM) nor the working paper are light bedtime reading. However, it's essential to have one of them close at hand if you hope to make optimum use of C++. If you can possibly stay awake, read one all the way through. If you can get a copy of the working paper, that is preferable to using the ARM.

Goldstein, Neil, and Jeff Alger. *Developing Object-Oriented Software for the Macintosh*. Reading, MA: Addison-Wesley, 1992. This book provides another excellent perspective on object-oriented design. It explodes some common myths. Don't let the title fool you—it's really not that specific to the Macintosh.

Hansen, Tony. *The C++ Answer Book*. Reading, MA: Addison-Wesley, 1990.

ISO/IEC. *ISO/IEC 9899:1990, International Standard for Information Systems— Programming Language C.* This is essentially the same as *ANSI C*, X3J11/88-159.

ISO/ANSI C++ Standardization Committee. "Working Paper for Draft Proposed American International Standard for Information Systems—Programming Language C++." This is essentially the same as the ANSI X3/J16 working paper for programming language C++.

Lampson, Butler. "Hints for Computer System Design" from the Proceedings of the Ninth ACM Symposium on Operating System Principles. *Operating System Review* 17, no. 1 (1983): 33–48. It's got lots of good observations by someone who's been through the wringer a few times.

Lippman, Stanley. *The C++ Primer.* 2d ed. Reading, MA: Addison-Wesley, 1991. A gentler tutorial for C++ than *The C++ Programming Language, 2nd Edition.* The second edition of Stroustrup's book is much better organized and is more approachable, lessening the need for this book. Also, this book does not cover classes until the later chapters.

Meyers, Scott. *Effective C++.* Reading, MA: Addison-Wesley, 1992. This book presents 50 good rules for designing and writing with C++. The intent of Meyers is not unlike that of *Taligent's Guide to Designing Programs.*

Murray, Robert B. *C++ Strategies and Tactics.* Reading, MA: Addison-Wesley, 1992. Many useful tips and techniques for using C++. Gives more detailed examples of some of the techniques discussed in this document.

Stroustrup, Bjarne. *The C++ Programming Language.* 2d ed. Reading, MA: Addison-Wesley, 1991. In addition to being the best introduction and reference to the language (excepting the ANSI draft specification), it includes excellent chapters on object-oriented design and management of object-oriented projects. These chapters are full of experience from the man who has seen more C++ projects than anyone else. However, this book is intimidating.

The 1987 Usenix C++ Conference Proceedings. USENIX Association, Berkeley CA.
The 1988 Usenix C++ Conference Proceedings. USENIX Association, Berkeley CA.
The 1990 Usenix C++ Conference Proceedings. USENIX Association, Berkeley CA.
The 1991 Usenix C++ Conference Proceedings. USENIX Association, Berkeley CA.
The 1992 Usenix C++ Conference Proceedings. USENIX Association, Berkeley CA.

Weinberg, Gerald. *The Psychology of Computer Programming.* New York, NY: Van Nostrand Reinhold, 1971. Some choice bits about what drives programmers to worry about efficiency.

Taligent is constantly looking for new books—please recommend your favorites.

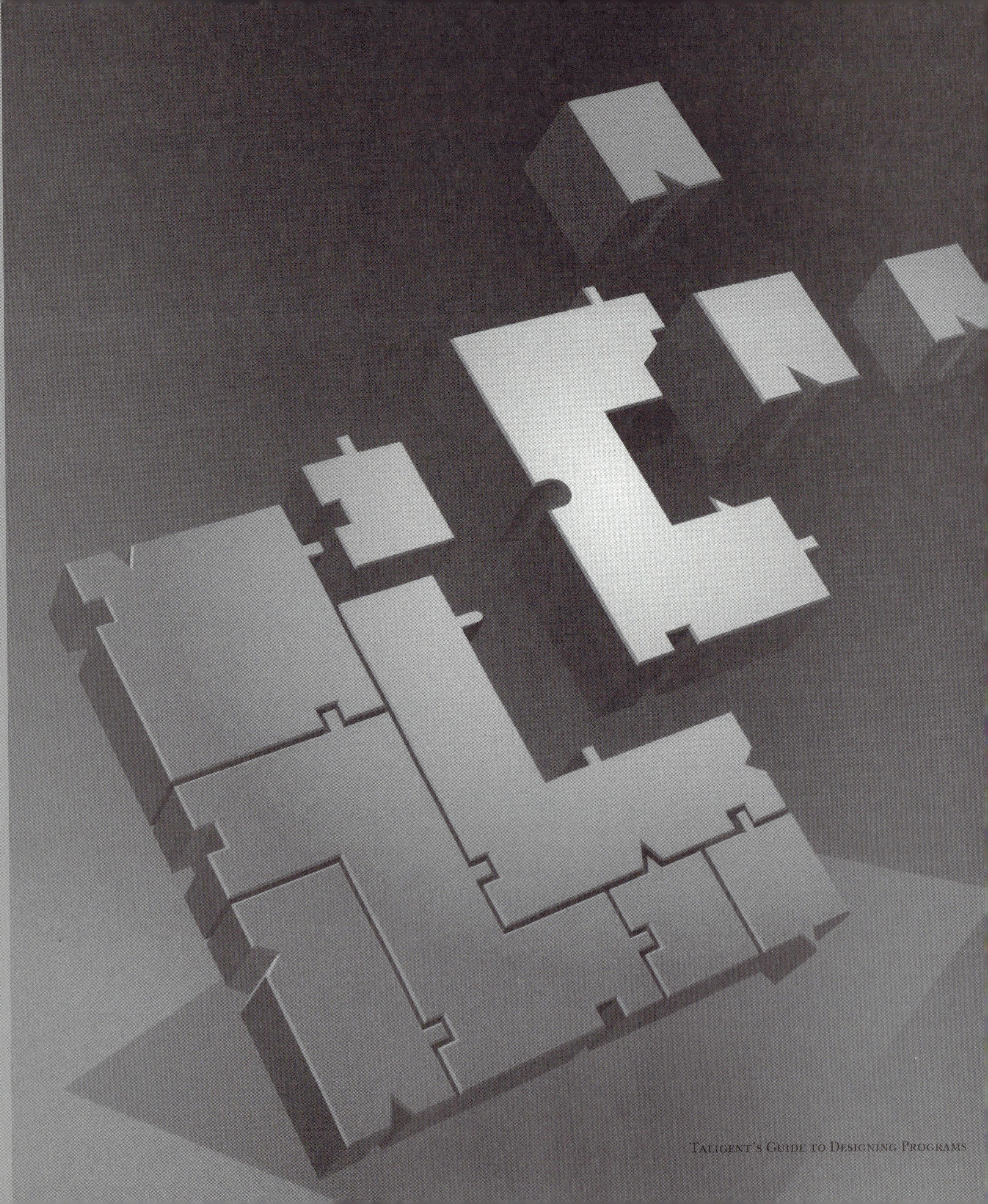

INDEX

D

dangling references, avoiding 94
data
    portability 112
    strip, cannot 58
data members
    arranging, adding, and removing 61
    importing and exporting with inlines 65
    naming conventions 33
data structures, interface issues 9
data types
    alignment restrictions 110
    C types, using 40, 41
    declaration conventions 40–43
    equality between different types 88
    exact definitions 110
    nonportable 113
    safe assumptions 109
    unsigned declarations 41
death, tracking 103
declarations in class scope 35
default argument implications 44
#define
    avoid symbolic constants 49
    enum instead 49
derived classes 15
    as arguments 15
designing
    guidelines and procedures 7
    invariants 10
destructor
    definition, required 11
    exception throwing 82
    virtual, making 71
device configuration objects 72
dictionaries, interface issues 9
double
    address assumptions 110
    always IEEE double-precision 110
downcasting 16
driver, installing 8
dynamic instantiation 104

E

Einstein, Albert 3
encapsulation issues 24
enum
    appear in class name space 36
    naming conventions 33
    type names local to class 50
    using 50
equality 86
error codes and conditions 74
exception handling 74–83
    assertions instead 83
    automatic objects, using 76
    checklist 74
    class design 81
    destructors, throwing 82
    interface specification 76
    passing exceptions 78
    recover, when to 83
    resource recovery 76
    syntax 75
    throwing 75
    when to signal 82
experimenting 20

F

file
    conventions 30
    float.h 110
    limits.h 41, 110
    PrimitiveTypes.h 41
    stddef.h 41
filenames
    case sensitivity 32
    code names, avoiding 31
final release and beyond 60
flags, using 53
flatten operator 113
float
    address assumptions 110
    always IEEE single-precision 110
float.h 110
frameworks 3
free 55

P

parameter
  caller should decide type 44
  name conventions 33
performance
  analysis 20
  canonical formats, accessing 112
  chunky iteration 21
  designing 19
  experiments 20
  inline functions, using 64
  issues 19
  static objects 20
  tracking time wasters 20
  using int not short 110
pointer
  arithmetic, avoiding 98
  arithmetic, how to 111
  avoid returning 45
  base class, casting 42
  counted 93
  counted, example of 97
  from a member function 24
  handling in C++ 46
  instead of references 46
  nil, deleting 106
  returning const 45
  treatment of 46
  untyped 111
  volatile, casting 42
  when to use 46
polymorphism
  cannot return a value 43
  definition 13
  design requirements 15
  instead of dynamic class instantiation 104
  multiple references, and 46
  requires
    base class 25
    public base classes 13
    virtual functions 67
  requiring pointers 47
  should accept references 44
  switches, instead of 72

portability
  bitwise operations 53
  designing for 109
  functions 67
  of data 112
portable hash 84
preemptive
  multitasking 99
  scheduling 99
preprocessor naming conventions 31
PrimitiveTypes.h 41
private
  base classes
    inherit behavior 13
    to avoid implementing exports 15
  functions, removing 61
  virtual functions 68
private
  always include 38
  state explicitly 38
processor
  dependent code 113
  mixed environments 112
PROSE 103
protected
  classes inherit behavior 13
  definitions, access to 14
protected, always state between public and private 38
protocol 15
ptrdiff_t
  nonportable 113
  useful for representing pointer differences 41
public, always state first in definition 38
pure virtual functions 67

Q

Quicksort 58

W